W9-ADN-907

Italian Aces
of World War 2

SERIES EDITOR: TONY HOLMES

OSPREY AIRCRAFT OF THE ACES • 34

Italian Aces of World War 2

Giovanni Massimello and Giorgio Apostolo

OSPREY
AVIATION

Front cover
On 19 August 1942, Tenente Pilota
Giulio Reiner was ordered to take-
off from his base at Fuka, not far
from El Alamein, with seven other
fighters (four from 73ª *Squadriglia*
and four from 96ª *Squadriglia*) to
intercept enemy aircraft which had
been identified over the frontline by
German *Freya* radar. Reiner's
wingman on this occasion was
Tenente Pilota Gibellini, who was
undertaking his first combat sortie.

Arriving over El Hamman at a
height of 6000 metres, the formation
spotted about 20 Hurricanes below
them carrying out strafing attacks.
While diving down to intercept the
fighter-bombers, Reiner noticed ten
Spitfires some 1000 metres above
his left wing, which were escorting
the Hurricanes. They immediately
turned towards the Italian formation
once the latter aircraft started to
dive. Reiner (followed by his flight)
quickly steepened his dive, before
throwing his fighter into a tight
banking left turn. As a result of this
high-g manoeuvre, he could now
see the underside of one of the
Spitfires.

'His nose filled three-quarters of
my gunsight', Reiner later recalled,
'and it was easy to hit him after a
short deflection shot to correct my
fire'. The Spitfire was mortally
damaged by the weight of the
Italian pilot's fire, giving Reiner his
third victory – and his first success
in the Macchi C.202. But the fight
did not end there, for the
inexperienced Ten Gibellini had
given chase to another Spitfire, and
by so doing had lost touch with his
leader. Finding himself alone, he
was swiftly shot down, despite the
late intervention of Reiner.

Four more Spitfires then turned
on the latter pilot, and he had to use
every ounce of his undoubted flying
skill to effect his escape. After finally
landing at Fuka, Reiner was
subsequently told by his
groundcrew that they had counted
107 bullet holes in his Macchi
fighter.

His victim during this sortie was
almost certainly future ten-kill
Spitfire ace Plt Off C J 'Sammy'
Samouelle of No 92 Sqn, who
successfully crash-landed his badly-
damaged Spitfire Vc trop (BR523)
behind the Allied frontline
(*cover artwork by Iain Wyllie*)

First published in Great Britain in 2000
by Osprey Publishing, Midland House, West Way, Botley, Oxford OX2 0PH, UK
443 Park Avenue South, New York, NY 10016, USA
E-mail: info@ospreypublishing.com

© 2000 Osprey Publishing
Reprinted 2002, 2004, 2005

ISBN 1 84176 078 1
A CIP catalogue record for this book is available from the British Library

Edited by Tony Holmes
Page design by TT Designs, T & B Truscott
Cover Artwork by Iain Wyllie
Text Translation, Aircraft Profiles and Scale Drawings by Richard Caruana
Origination by Grasmere Digital Imaging, Leeds, UK
Printed through Bookbuilders, Hong Kong

EDITOR'S NOTE
To make this best-selling series as authoritative as possible, the Editor would
be interested in hearing from any individual who may have relevant
photographs, documentation or first-hand experiences relating to the aces,
and their aircraft, of the various theatres of war. Any material used will be
credited to its original source. Please write to Tony Holmes at 16 Sandilands,
Sevenoaks, Kents, TN13 2SP, Great Britain, or contact the Editor
by e-mail at: tony.holmes@osprey-jets.freeserve.co.uk

For a catalogue of all titles published by Osprey Publishing please contact us at:
NORTH AMERICA
Osprey Direct, 2427 Bond Street, University Park, IL 60466, USA
E-mail: info@ospreydirectusa.com
ALL OTHER REGIONS
Osprey Direct UK, P.O. Box 140, Wellingborough, Northants, NN8 2FA, UK
E-mail: info@ospreydirect.co.uk
www.ospreypublishing.com

Back cover
Seen standing with his hands in his pockets at Mirafiori, east of the
Franco-Italian border, in mid-1940, 18º *Gruppo's* Maresciallo Felice Longhi
had scored a single kill in Spain during the civil war. He would claim a further
five victories during World War 2, all with 95ª *Squadriglia*. CR.42 '95-5'
was Longhi's personal mount

CONTENTS

INTRODUCTION

By VE-Day the Italian public was in no mood to share in the victory celebrations enjoyed by the Allies. In contrast with World War 1, when returning servicemen were accorded the highest accolades associated with their victory in that conflict, a veil was drawn over the events, and men, who had fought in a war full of painful memories for all Italians. Fighting a civil war for the last 18 months of World War 2, which brought five years of conflict to a tragic and bitter end, the deep psychological wounds suffered by all Italians took decades to heal. Even today, almost 60 years after the end of hostilities, some aspects of the Italian participation in World War 2 are still looked upon suspiciously, and thus prove difficult to tackle objectively.

The subject of this book is one area that has, in the past, been problematic to research. As far as recognising Italian fighter pilots as 'aces', there existed within official quarters a tacit agreement not to deal with a matter some feared could possibly reopen old wounds. A case in point was the official treatment of those airmen who had fought alongside the Germans after the Armistice of 8 September 1943. Far from making a political choice to fight on with their former ally, most pilots were simply caught on the northern side of the frontline when the Armistice came into effect – admittedly, some still harboured strong feelings towards the Germans, whom they had fought alongside since 1940.

Though knowing full well the hopelessness of pursuing a lost war, these individuals continued to fight gallantly in defence of northern Italian skies. And once the conflict was over, these unquestionably brave pilots were effectively put on trial and duly expelled from the post-war air force. Among their number were some of the most successful Italian aces of World War 2.

This singular event explains why the Historical Section of the Italian Air Force has politely, but consistently, ignored requests from both local and foreign researchers for information relating to Italian fighter aces of World War 2. Either including or excluding the names of the pilots who remained supportive of the Axis cause would have caused an unacceptable political problem for those in officialdom, so no 'official' list of Italian aces – or even a comprehensive record of confirmed 'claims' – has ever been issued by the Italian Air Force.

As a result of this policy, the work presented within this volume represents many years of personal research on the part of the authors, and we have made every effort to carefully check all the combat accounts featured with primary sources.

We hope that this book will be considered as a small, but concrete, contribution to the preservation of the memory of those men whose exploits must not be forgotten by present and future generations.

Giovanni Massimello & Giorgio Apostolo
Milan
August 2000

ITALIAN AIR WAR

taly's part in the air war during World War 2 is often overlooked and undervalued, especially in English- and German-language publications. It can be argued that the *Regia Aeronautica's* contribution during the three years it was embroiled in conflict (10 June 1940 to 8 September 1943) as an ally of Germany was of little strategic importance. Indeed, its efforts in the major campaigns such as the Battle of Britain and the invasion of the Soviet Union were absolutely marginal.

With the dissolution of the old *Regia Aeronautica* following the Armistice, the Italian air force effectively split into two opposing camps. The *Aeronautica Co-Belligerante* (Co-Belligerant Air Force) to the south fought on the side of the Allies, and the *Aeronautica Nazionale Repubblicana* (ANR) in the north remained in the frontline alongside the Germans. Like the *Regia Aeronautica* before them, both forces proved to be of little strategic value to their respective allies.

However, it is not fair, or accurate, to dismiss the entire wartime efforts of Italian aviators as unimportant. Those fighting in the Mediterranean and North Africa, in particular, proved to be worthy foes for the Allies, with the *Regia Aeronautica* not being afforded a moment's respite between 11 June 1940 and 12 May 1943, firstly in Libya and then Tunisia.

Proof of the overall dismissal of the Italian fighter force in particular by many historians can be seen in the fact that the Messerschmitt Bf 109 is often recorded as being the sole Axis fighter protagonist in the aerial battles fought over the desert from late 1942 onwards. In actuality, units equipped with the Macchi C.202 were constantly present, and made a significant contribution.

Moreover, it is unfair to forget the courage and determination displayed by those men who continued to fight despite being totally outnumbered in the air, and suffering from poor logistical support on the ground. Aviators that sacrificed their lives in combat did so fully conscious of a sense of duty, animated by a sincere love for their country.

This Macchi C.200 from the first production series (fitted with a sliding canopy) belongs to 1° *Stormo*. This unit earned fame pre-war due to its brilliant aerobatic displays. Having enjoyed many years of flying agile biplane fighters, Italian pilots did not initially welcome the arrival of Macchi's less manoeuvrable C.200 in the frontline

THE FIGHTER WAR

When Italy entered the war on 10 June 1940, it was completely unprepared to fight a long conflict. Fully aware of this situation, officials from all government ministries associated with the armed forces tried to dissuade *Il Duce*, Benito Mussolini, from taking such a monumental decision. However, he was convinced that a German victory was only a matter of weeks away following the *Blitzkrieg* in the west, and that the prize for joining the Axis alliance would be his share in the spoils of war. What actually happened not only disproved *Il Duce's* theory, but also highlighted shortcomings in both military preparedness and weaponry.

Despite basking in the glory of victorious campaigns in Ethiopia and Spain, and having performed numerous record flights in the inter-war years that proved both the soundness of its aircraft and skill of its pilots, the *Regia Aeronautica* was as unready to fight as either the army or navy. The Italian public, and the world at large, thought otherwise, however, thanks to a well-orchestrated publicity campaign which had over-emphasised its technical and operational capabilities.

The *Regia Aeronautica's* shortcomings had first been exposed during its 'successful' foray into Spain in support of General Franco's Nationalist forces in the recent bloody civil war. Considerable resources in terms of both men and machinery had been expended, depleting its frontline capabilities, slowing down aircraft development and impeding training. Even the two success stories of the war, the S.79 bomber (none of which were downed by Republican fighters in three years of war) and the CR.32 biplane fighter, only helped instill in the *Regia Aeronautica* a false sense of security in obsolescent designs.

The Italian aviation industry pointed to the proven combat ability of its products, although in reality these successes only served to delay the implemetation of proper techniques of mass-production as were in place in Britain, Germany and the USA. By and large, designers and builders were proud of their 'artisan' productions, inspired by the aerobatic prowess of Italian pilots. Moreover, strategic considerations dictated that bombers were more important than other types. This mission doctrine was advocated by Mussolini himself, who envisioned a *Blitzkrieg* victory in which fighters would be of marginal importance.

The direct result of this belief was that on the day Italy declared war, there were 24 *stormi* of bombers in the *Regia Aeronautica* and only eight of fighters. The latter were, in the main, equipped with Fiat

This CR.42 bears the markings of 2° *Stormo's* 93ª *Squadriglia*. Although obsolete in comparison with the monoplane fighters of the day, the Fiat did enjoy some success against RAF Gladiators and Blenheims during the opening months of the North African campaign. Indeed, 77ª *Squadriglia's* Tenente Giulio Torresi succeeded in scoring his first six (of ten) victories up to Christmas 1940

A trio of 3° *Stormo* C.202s prepare to taxy out from their makeshift dispersal at Tauorga, on the Libyan coast, in early January 1943. The aircraft in the foreground carries the *Baracca* script just aft of the propeller, denoting that it had been passed on to 3° *Stormo* by 4° *Stormo* when the latter unit returned to Italy early in late 1942

This line-up of C.200s from 76ª *Squadriglia* (7° *Gruppo*, 54° *Stormo*) was photographed at Pantelleria in the spring of 1942. The *squadriglia*, which at that time was led by Capitano Calistri (three individual victories), was later commanded by Capitano Visconti, who obtained his first six kills with this unit

CR.42 biplanes. All-metal monoplanes such as the Macchi C.200 and Fiat G.50 were undoubtedly far superior to the Fiat biplane fighter, despite being undergunned and underpowered in comparison with other fighters from Germany, Britain and the USA. Yet the C.200 and G.50 were generally disliked by frontline pilots, who refused to adapt their tactics to better suit the faster, but less agile, monoplane fighters. Instead, they insisted on persevering with antiquated tactics based on precision aerobatics, which were identical to those used by the Italian Air Corps against the Austro-Hungarians during World War 1.

The combination of the Italian aviation industry's inability to cope with series production of modern, stressed-skinned monoplane fighters, and the reluctance of frontline units to employ such aircraft effectively meant that Italian fighter development lagged some way behind other industrialised nations come 1940. The first aerial actions involving the *Regia Aeronautica* fully exposed these weaknesses.

Boasting a modest industrial infrastructure in comparison with both its allies and its enemies, Italy faced great problems in implementing a crash programme of frontline modernisation. Proof of this was that Macchi's C.202 (the first truly modern Italian-designed and built monoplane fighter) did not make its operational debut until the autumn of 1941. With only meagre quantities of Macchi fighters made available to the *Regia Aeronautica*, the C.202 had little real impact on the North African air war. So slow was the production of this fighter that entire frontline units (such as 8° *Gruppo*) were still flying the long-obsolete C.200 when the Armistice was signed in September 1943.

As alluded to earlier in this chapter, it was not only the equipment that failed to come up to scratch when the *Regia Aeronautica* was committed to combat. Serious shortcomings in the operational abilities of its fighter pilots were also cruelly exposed, pointing directly to a failure in the pre-war training programme. Two areas of particular weakness were aerial gunnery and instrument navigation flying. Furthermore, ground-to-air and air-to-air radio communication aids, not to mention radar, were practically non-existent within the *Regia Aeronautica*.

Taking all this into consideration, it is not difficult to understand why Italian pilots were at a disadvantage when they confronted the enemy (essentially the RAF). Yet despite these technical and tactical problems, when fighting on even terms, such as in East Africa and, for a short time, in North Africa, Italian fighter pilots more than held their own. Proof, if ever it was needed, that valour was one commodity far from lacking within the fighter force of the *Regia Aeronautica*.

THEATRES OF WAR

In the spring of 1940, realising that war was not far away, senior officers within the *Regia Aeronautica* prepared the operational plan PR 12 in co-ordination with the other branches of the Italian armed forces. As a part of this strategy, in the week preceding 10 June 1940, units had taken up their respective positions as instructed in PR 12.

At that time the air force's total strength consisted of 3269 aircraft, of which only 1795 were deemed to be combat-effective. These were split between 25 bomber *stormi*, eight fighter *stormi*, one assault *stormo* and two combat *gruppi*. A handful of additional combat types were also used by observation and maritime reconnaissance units.

The disposition of fighter units as of 10 June 1940 was as follows:

1ª *Squadra Aerea*

3º *Stormo*	CR.42	18º *Gruppo*	Novi Ligure e Albenga
		23º *Gruppo*	Cervere
53º *Stormo*	CR.42	150º *Gruppo*	Caselle Torinese
		151º *Gruppo*	Casablanca
54º *Stormo*	C.200	152º *Gruppo*	Airasca
		153º *Gruppo*	Vergiate
9º *Gruppo*	CR.42		Gorizia

2ª *Squadra Aerea*

1º *Stormo*	CR.42/CR.32	17º *Gruppo*	Palermo
		157º *Gruppo*	Trapani
6º *Gruppo Autonomo*	C.200		Catania

3ª *Squadra Aerea*

51º *Stormo*	G.50	20º *Gruppo*	Ciampino
21º *Gruppo*			
52º *Stormo*	G.50/CR.32	22º *Gruppo*	Pontedera
24º *Gruppo*			Sarzana

4ª *Squadra Aerea*

2º *Gruppo Autonomo*	CR.32		Grottaglie

Aeronautica della Sardegna

3º *Gruppo Autonomo*	CR.32		Monserrato

Aeronautica dell'Albania

160º *Gruppo Autonomo*	CR.32		Tirana

Aeronautica dell'Egeo

163ª *Squadriglia Autonomo*	CR.32		Rodi

Aeronautica della Libia

2º *Stormo*	CR.42/CR.32	13º *Gruppo*	Castelbenito
	CR.32	8º *Gruppo*	Tobruk T2
10º *Gruppo*	CR.32		Tobruk T2

Aeronautica dell'AOI

410ª *Squadriglia Autonomo*	CR.32		Giggiga

411ª *Squadriglia Autonomo*	CR.32	Dire Daua
412ª *Squadriglia Autonomo*	CR.42	Gora
413ª *Squadriglia Autonomo*	CR.42	Assab

This frontline force totalled some 77 C.200s, 88 G.50s, 200 CR.42s and 177 CR.32s that were deemed to be fully operational. A further 165 fighters were not considered combat ready, whilst an additional 287 were either having problems rectified at Macchi or Fiat, or were undergoing routine servicing.

CAMPAIGN ACROSS THE ALPS

The Italian involvement in the defeat of France lasted a mere two weeks, and although the *Regia Aeronautica* possessed an adequate number of bombers at the start of hostilities, directives from high command prescribed that 'a close defensive strategy was to be adopted on land, air and in all sectors'. No action, therefore, was contemplated against Corsica, northern France or Tunisia.

The units involved in the minor actions that took place in this theatre in late June 1940 included three *stormi* from 1ª *Squadra Aerea*, two of which – 3º and 53º – were equipped with CR.42s. The latter units each boasted two *gruppi* of three *squadriglie* (over 100 aircraft), whilst the third *gruppo* was the newly-formed 54º, flying C.200s.

Units in the south such as 1º *Stormo* at Palermo (CR.42s and CR.32s), 6º *Gruppo Autonomo* at Catania (C.200), 51º *Stormo* at Ciampino (G.50s) and 52º at Capodichino (G.50s and CR.32s) also saw limited action, as did 6º *Stormo* (CR.32), split between Monserrato and Alghero, in Sardinia.

Those units committed to combat had the task of indirectly protecting bomber *gruppi* flying BR.20s at high altitude. When flying at lower altitudes fighter aircraft were directed to strafe ground targets, with the overall objective being to neutralise French airfields in Provence. Such attacks by CR.42s of 3º *Stormo* and 151º *Gruppo* proved effective, although the French soon realised that their Dewoitine D.520 and Morane MS.406 monoplane fighters were technically superior. Indeed, although totally out-numbered by their Italian foes, the French pilots came out on top in the few aerial encounters that took place between the much slower, and lightly-armed, Italian biplanes and the D.520s and MS.406s.

The most important clash of this campaign took place on 15 June, when 12 CR.42s from the 23º *Gruppo* met six D.520s from the fifth squadron of GC III/6. The Italian formation was taken by surprise and failed to form a defensive circle in time, resulting in two Fiat fighters being swiftly shot down by Adjutant Pierre Le Gloan, vice-commander of the French unit. He then came across a second formation over Hyéres and destroyed another Italian aircraft. The fighting did not end there, however, as when the French pilot arrived back at his base he found that it was being attacked by more CR.42s. With a short burst of cannon fire he shot down Capitano Luigi Filippi, CO of 75ª *Squadriglia*, thus making Le Gloan an 'ace in a day' (see *Osprey Aircraft of the Aces 28 - French Aces of World War 2* for further details).

French aircraft also mounted a bombing raid against Turin, the night operation by the *Armeé de l'Air* causing the *Regia Aeronautica* to form its first nightfighter unit, based at Ciampino airport in Rome. Equipped with three CR.32s fitted with extended exhaust pipes to shield engine exhaust flames, the small band of fighters was designated the *Sezione Caccia Notturna* (night fighter flight).

During the short campaign on the Western Front, Italian fighter pilots completed 1770 flying hours and performed 11 strafing attacks. They were also credited with downing ten French aircraft.

CHANNEL FRONT

As part of the planned German invasion of Britain (codenamed Operation *Sealion*) in the late summer of 1940, the *Corpo Aereo Italiano* (CAI) arrived in Belgium in mid-October to lend its Axis partner material support. Convinced of a German victory, Benito Mussolini had personally insisted upon the hasty despatch of the CAI in order to guarantee an Italian presence during what he considered to be the final phase of the war. However, by the time the *corpo* arrived on the Channel Front the invasion had been postponed indefinitely, and the RAF had effectively won the Battle of Britain.

The CAI consisted of 13° and 43° *Stormi*, with 38 and 37 twin-engined BR.20s respectively, and 18° and 20° *Gruppi*, equipped with 50 CR.42s and 48 G.50s (the fighter units were controlled by 56° *Stormo Caccia*). Five Cant Z.1007s also joined the *corpo* to fulfil the reconnaissance mission.

None of the Italian fighter or bomber types were suited to combat in this theatre, being markedly inferior to their contemporaries within both the RAF and the Luftwaffe. The growing onset of winter further exacerbated the inadequacies of the equipment, and problems were first experienced during the series of ferry flights undertaken between Italy and Belgium. On 19 October, when all the units had finally managed to reach their base at Ursel, fighter readiness had already decreased to 42 G.50s and 47 CR.42s – and it should be remembered that the latter type lacked radio equipment!

Despite myriad problems, the CAI completed its first mission on the night of 25 October when the BR.20s bombed Harwich. Four days later, a day raid was mounted by 15 bombers, escorted by 70 fighters. On 11 November an audacious daylight attack was carried out that saw the Z.1007s perform a diversionary raid on Great Yarmouth while ten BR.20s, escorted by 40 CR.42s, attempted to hit Harwich, in conjunction with German Ju 87s.

Intercepted by Hurricanes, the Italian formation lost three bombers and three fighters, while a further three damaged BR.20s

Following a brief campaign against France, the *Regia Aeronautica's* only other contribution to the war on the Western Front was the less than successful expeditionary force sent to Belgium in late October 1940 to participate in the Battle of Britain. Contrary to propaganda claims issued at the time, the results achieved over southern England and East Anglia were extremely modest. This photo shows an 18° *Gruppo* CR.42 (with Tenente Giulio Cesare Giuntella at the controls) in Belgium running up prior to flying a bomber escort mission

crash-landed outside their airfield. The fighters had had to beat a hasty retreat when they had run low on fuel, 19 of them also landing away from their home base. This was the last daylight bombing operation undertaken by CAI units, which subsequently flew only night sorties. Another clash between British and Italian fighters took place on 23 November when 29 CR.42s flew an offensive sweep along the Channel coast

between Ramsgate and Folkestone. Intercepted by 20 RAF fighters, the *Regia Aeronautica* lost two aircraft.

This view was taken at Ursel, in Belgium, on the same occasion as the photo featured on the previous page. Immediately in front of the CR.42 in the foreground is the aircraft flown by 18° *Gruppo's* CO, Maggiore Ferruccio Vosilla. A veteran of the Spanish Civil War, his fighter wears a command pennant beneath its cockpit

The Italian contribution to the fight on the Channel Front came to an end on 3 January 1941, CAI units having already begun to pack up their equipment and prepare for the ferry flight home at the end of December. Its withdrawal was supposed to have been only a temporary measure due to poor weather, but in actuality the decision to remove the CAI was taken on account of the worsening situation for Italian forces both on the Greek Front and in North Africa.

A handful of G.50s from 352ª and 353ª *Squadriglie* remained in Belgium until the spring, flying defensive patrols between Dunkirk and Calais. RAF fighters were spotted only once during this time, and no contact was established. On 15 April the G.50s were ordered back to Ciampino, bringing to a close the Channel Front campaign.

During the few bombing missions flown by the CAI, BR.20s and Z.1007s had dropped a total of 54 tons of ordnance on England. In support of these operations, the two fighter *gruppi* had completed 883 sorties, losing nine aircraft (and a further nine damaged) in combat.

GREECE AND ALBANIA

On 28 October 1940, *Il Duce* ordered his forces to conduct a surprise invasion of nearby Greece after issuing the government of the latter country with an ultimatum alleging a list of 'wrongs' perpetrated by the Greeks against Italy.

Apart from missions against ports and logistics centres, Italian fighters were only involved in sporadic engagements with Greek aircraft in the first few days of the invasion. However, fighting intensified with the arrival of the first RAF assets in-theatre in early November. On the 19th, for example, nine Gloster Gladiators of No 80 Sqn, led by three Greek PZL P.24 fighters, bounced a flight of CR.42s from 160° *Gruppo* and G.50s from 24° *Gruppo*. In the battle that ensued, three biplane fighters and a single G.50 were shot down for the loss of a solitary Gladiator (with a further two RAF fighters claimed as probables).

By the end of November additional units had become available in the south of Italy, including C.200-equipped 373ª and 374ª *Squadriglie*. Both units soon found themselves engaging Hurricanes that had arrived from Egypt in an effort to bolster the Greek Air Force.

A major success for the fighters was obtained on 21 December when 15 CR.42s clashed with ten No 80 Sqn Gladiators over the Italian frontline. RAF pilots subsequently claimed to have destroyed eight CR.42s and the Italians nine Gladiators, although in actuality both sides lost two fighters apiece.

The *Regia Aeronautica* was kept under continuous pressure by the enemy through to the spring of 1941, and it abandoned several advanced Albanian airfields. However, other sites further north remained in Italian hands, with

154º *Gruppo* flying from Berat, 394ª *Squadriglia* operating out of Devoli, 150º *Gruppo* from Valona and 24º *Gruppo* split between Scutari and Tirana.

The RAF presence in Greece continued to grow as 1941 wore on, forcing the *Regia Aeronautica* to fly numerous patrols in an attempt to intercept and engage enemy bombers. However, the intervention of German forces in early April halted the Allied push into Albania, allowing an Italian air offensive to be launched against both Greece and Yugoslavia. In order to be better prepared for the renewed fighting in the Balkans, 150º *Gruppo* replaced its CR.42s with C.200s, whilst other units were transferred to Albanian airfields, including 371º *Gruppo* with ten C.200s and 22º *Gruppo* with 36 Macchi fighters.

Now fighting well-equipped, and battle-hardened, Wehrmacht and Luftwaffe units, supported by an increased Italian force, the Greeks requested an armistice on 27 April 1941 – by which time the bloody 11-day war with Yugoslavia had also come to an end.

Notwithstanding the high number of sorties flown by the *Regia Aeronautica's* fighter force (some 14,000, totalling over 21,000 flying hours), results were rather modest, with considerable losses being inflicted on the *gruppi* committed to the Balkans campaign.

EAST AFRICA

When Italy declared war on France and Britain, the air force units based in *Africa Orientale Italiana* (AOI – Italian East Africa) found

A pilot from 160º *Gruppo* is helped on with his parachute prior to flying a sortie over Greece in late 1940. The unit's three *squadriglie* (393ª, 394ª and 395ª) all distinguished themselves during the bitterly fought Greek campaign, flying from bases in Albania. Among the *gruppo's* foremost pilots were Capitano Eber Giudice, Tenente Giuliano Fissore and Sergente Manfredo Bianchi. Note that this CR.42 (like all the others in 394ª *Squadriglia*) features *Il Duce's* profile painted ahead of the standard fuselage fascio marking

Sharing fighter duties with the ubiquitous CR.42 on the Greek-Albanian Front was the G.50, these examples belonging to 354ª *Squadriglia* (154º *Gruppo Autonomo*). The fighter in the foreground wears the unit badge at the base of its fin, the Roman motto that ran around the edge of the circular emblem reading *'Fatte vede che ridemo'* ('Show up so we can have a laugh')

themselves in an unenviable position. Practically cut off from home, and surrounded by colonial territories controlled by the enemy, *Regia* units were also, in the main, equipped with obsolescent aircraft types.

On 10 June 1940, the *Regia Aeronautica* in AOI boasted a total force of 323 aeroplanes, 81 of which were classified unserviceable. The fighter force within the AOI boiled down to 14 CR.42s and 32 CR.32s, split into four *squadriglie*. Opposing the Italians

The *Regia Aeronautica's* fighter force in East Africa consisted entirely of Fiat biplanes. This captured CR.42 displays the theatre markings, which consisted of a black cross of St Andrew on a white square. This 413ª *Squadriglia* aircraft (along with a CR.32 – possibly MM 4191) was flown back to South Africa in August 1941 following its capture in Ethiopia. Put on public display, both Fiat fighters survived through to the end of the war, although only small parts of the CR.32 can be seen on display in the South African Air Force (SAAF) Museum today. Note the SAAF Lockheed Lodestar parked in the background

were British and Commonwealth units equipped with 370 aircraft which, like those flown by the *Regia Aeronautica*, were principally older types. However, a few dozen Hurricanes and Blenheims were also in-theatre, and unlike the Italians, the Allies could rely on reinforcements.

Taking the initiative, the Italians immediately seized British Somaliland, with the *Regia Aeronautica* achieving mastery of the skies by destroying a good number of Allied aircraft on the ground at Burao, La Faruk and Hergheisa. The Italians were even so bold as to attack convoys as far afield as the Red Sea, and it was during one of these operations, on 11 February 1941, that 17-kill ace Capitano Mario Visentini was killed when he flew his CR.42 into Mount Nefasit whilst looking for a fellow pilot.

In the early spring of 1941 Allied forces in-theatre were improved with the arrival of more modern aircraft. However, for the Italians supplies were becoming increasingly difficult to come by. Indeed, when an additional 50 CR.42s were sent to the AOI, the only way to ensure their arrival was to fly them in disassembled in the holds of Savoia-Marchetti S.82 tri-motor transports. When the British launched their new offensive in late April 1941, only two S.79s, four Caproni Ca.113s, five CR.42 and a single CR.32 remained serviceable in the whole of Italian-held East Africa. With the surrender of the Amba Alagi garrison on 19 May, effective Italian resistance in-theatre ended.

However, in western Ethiopia the last vestiges of the *Regia Aeronautica* in the AOI continued to fly sporadically from Gondar in support of ground troops until the last CR.42 was burnt, in November 1941, to prevent its capture by the Allies. No fewer than seven Italian aces were created during the near 18 months of fighting in the AOI.

NORTH AFRICA

The aerial fighting in the North African campaign was almost always linked to the land battles being fought along the desolate Mediterranean coastline of Libya, Egypt and, finally, Tunisia. It never effectively developed a strategic character of its own, and fighter pilots (and all other pilots in-theatre for that matter) waged war apace with the humble soldier on the ground, preceding his advance or being sacrificed to cover his retreat. It was in North Africa, however, that Italian pilots obtained the majority of their victories.

Upon the Italian declaration of war, the *Regia Aeronautica's* sole fighter presence in Libya consisted of the CR.42-equipped 10º *Gruppo* at Benina and 13º *Gruppo* at Castelbenito. Older CR.32s remained in service alongside the CR.42s (25 with 8º *Gruppo* and 11 with 13º *Gruppo*), although these had been relegated to ground attack duties.

Seeking to eradicate the modest Italian force in North Africa before it became large enough to pose a real threat, the handful of RAF fighter units based in neighbouring Egypt attempted to seize control of the skies by introducing a small number of Hurricanes into service within days of Italy entering the war. However, these were never sufficient in number to deal with the Fiat fighters, and both sides simply skirmished until 13 September 1940. On this date Marshal Rodolfo Graziani (who had taken over command in Libya after the death of Italo Balbo on 28 June) ordered his army to cross the Egyptian border and head east for Suez. Within a week his troops had got as far as Sidi Barrani, where Graziani stopped to plan his next offensive.

In early December the Marshal considered that the time was right for Italian forces to push forward to ensure the capture of Marsa Matruh. However, his progress was stymied by a sudden 'limited five-day offensive' launched by Field Marshal Sir Archibald Wavell and General Sir Richard O'Connor. This 'limited' campaign ended with the capture of Cyrenaica (now eastern Libya) by the Allies!

On the eve of that attack, 5ª *Squadra Aerea* could muster 444 aircraft, of which 324 were fully serviceable. On the British side, the RAF boasted roughly the same number of aircraft, although its fighter force now featured more Hurricanes than it had done in the autumn.

The British counter-attack was as sudden as it was effective, and it caused the German high command such concern that X *Fliegerkorps* hastily left Sicily in late January 1941 to help shore up the routed Italian forces. Indeed, 5ª *Squadra Aerea* had been practically wiped out during December's fighting, and the following month replacement aircraft in the form of the first monoplane fighters to reach North Africa arrived at Castelbenito. These consisted of 37 G.50s from 2º *Gruppo Autonomo* (150ª, 151ª and 152ª *Squadriglia*), together with 358ª *Squadriglia* from 52º *Stormo's* 22º *Gruppo*. At the end of January a further two G.50-equipped *gruppi* – 20º (from Belgium) and 155º – were sent to Libya.

The arrival of the Germans, and General Erwin Rommel in particular, helped raise Italian morale, which had been completely shattered. Fighting recommenced, although at a much reduced level, with the handful of *Fliegerfuhrer Afrika* units seeing the bulk of the action. Due to its lack of modern aircraft, 5ª *Squadra Aerea* could only manage a limited contribu-

For first phase of the North African campaign (June-December 1940), the principal Italian fighter in-theatre was the CR.42. One of the units heavily involved in the fighting was 9° *Gruppo* (4° *Stormo*), whose Fiat biplanes are seen here patrolling in strength. The aircraft nearest to the camera belongs to *gruppo* commander Maggiore Ernesto Botto 'Gamba di Ferro', who was decorated with a Gold Medal following his service in Spain. Despite losing a leg in the latter campaign, he had returned to frontline flying by 1940. Botto, who claimed four kills in Spain, scored a further three victories during World War 2

tion to the new Axis offensive, its aircraft flying mainly by night.

Italian fighters did, however, see much service escorting German Ju 87s into combat. And it was during the spring-summer of 1941 that co-operation between Italian and German forces began to flourish, especially at unit level. Such co-operation was recorded in the following report drawn up by Maggiore Baylon, then commander of a fighter unit equipped with G.50s;

'As from 23 April 1941, my 2º *Gruppo Autonomo*, detached at base No 1 north of Derna, initiated a period of co-operation with *X CAT* (*X Fliegerkorps*) by flying (mainly) escort missions to Ju 87s bombing besieged Tobruk, as well as other enemy forces at Sollum-Halfaya Pass and Ridotta Capuzzo, and Ju 88s attacking ships out at sea. I have flown 51 escort missions for German aircraft between 23 April and 6 July. For each mission we used 12 to 18 G.50s. This proved to be an excellent operational period thanks to the precision and skill with which each mission was planned by *X CAT* command.'

Fighter units were replenished throughout the summer of 1941 with new aircraft in an effort to keep pace with attrition, while at the same time new units were transferred in from Italy. One such outfit was C.200-equipped 153º *Gruppo*, which arrived in Castelbenito on 2 July.

The second British counter-offensive of the campaign, codenamed *Crusader*, was launched in the early hours of 18 November 1941, and one of the first Axis units to feel the direct effects of this was 20º *Gruppo*. Having flown from Martuba to the transit airfield at Sidi Rezegh to escort a formation of fighter-bombers on an early-morning mission, the unit's G.50s were caught on the ground by a Long Range Desert Group patrol which had succeeded in driving some 80 kilometres into Italian-held territory without being detected! Only three G.50s managed to scramble to safety, leaving a further 18 destroyed by enemy fire on the ground. The unit returned to Italy soon afterwards.

By early January 1942 the British had advanced halfway across Libya to El Agheila, although their planned conquest of the whole of the country was thwarted when Rommel counter-attacked on the 21st of the month. All available fighter units were launched to harry the retreating Allied troops, and by 29 January Axis forces had reoccupied Benghasi, where 6º and 150º *Gruppi* took up residence. 8º *Gruppo* also advanced eastwards to El Agheila and 3º *Gruppo* to Sidi el Ahmar.

On 30 January the 8th Army commander (Ritchie) decided to retire behind the Gazala line which

Operating CR.42s alongside 9° *Gruppo* within 4° *Stormo* in 1940 was 10° *Gruppo*, whose 91ª *Squadriglia* is seen here in Libya. The unit's griffin emblem can just be seen on the mainwheel fairing of the aircraft closest to the camera. The fighter also wears the 10° *Gruppo* badge (Baracca's black horse) on its rear fuselage – note that 9° *Gruppo* also used this marking, but with the colours reversed. Finally, all three fighters visible in this shot have white-painted upper wingtips, which was the theatre marking adopted by the *Regia Aeronautica* to facilitate rapid identification of friendly aircraft in North Africa

G.50s first appeared in Libya during the spring of 1941, this particular example hailing from 20° *Gruppo* (which was operating autonomously at the time). It features the yellow-painted cowling applied to all Italian fighters (and some reconnaissance and bomber types) operating in North Africa from late 1940 onwards. This practice was officially discontinued in October 1941, after which yellow theatre markings were only retained on aircraft assigned to the Eastern Front

led north to the coastal fortifications at Tobruk. Undaunted, Rommel continued his chase, directing all aerial forces to soften up the port stronghold. German bombers carried out the bulk of these attacks in daylight hours, relying on C.200s and C.202s to provide fighter escort. During one such mission, Italian Deputy Chief of Staff Generale Santoro recorded;

C.202s of 9° *Gruppo* are hastily pushed away from a blazing Macchi fighter that has just crash-landed at the unit's Martuba base in late 1941. Groundcrewmen can be seen trying to manhandle the aircraft at left away from the blazing fighter, whilst a pilot dashes towards the C.202 at the right of the shot

'Ten C.200s, which were providing close escort for 12 Ju 87s, were attacked by 20 P-40s. Bf 109s, covering them from afar, failed to come to their assistance for some reason. The Italian pilots took up the overwhelming challenge, fighting to their limits, and enabling the German formation to return home unharmed – at the cost of six C.200s.'

The Italo-German offensive to break through the Gazala-Bir Hachiem line recommenced on 26 May 1942, when 59 C.202s carried out a surprise dawn attack on the large Allied airfield at Gambut. A formation of 24 Kittyhawks was found neatly parked wing-to-wing on the ground, and these were duly attacked. Although the Italian pilots claimed to have 'wiped out' the Allied fighters, RAF records shows that just two No 250 Sqn Kittyhawks were reportedly damaged.

When the Axis armoured divisions launched their attack in the afternoon, C.200s and CR.42s, together with Luftwaffe units, hit British forces behind their fortified lines. Finally, that evening, after some 800 Italian and German aircraft had attacked Tobruk, the beleaguered stronghold finally surrendered.

Following the fall of Tobruk, Axis troops kept the pressure on retreating Allied forces, at times advancing as much as 50 kilometres in a day. Air support now entered a critical phase, for ground equipment could not be transferred to advanced airfields at the same rate as mechanised troops were heading eastward. Moreover, the movement of troops hindered proper logistical co-operation, which, in truth, had never been properly planned by either the Italians or the Germans.

Fortunately, the RAF failed to put in much of an appearance during the headlong Allied retreat, leaving the vulnerable Axis ground columns to go about their business practically undisturbed. Equally, Axis units never really exploited the grave situation that now faced the Allies, allowing the retreat to continue in an orderly manner. In such circumstance, had the full weight of Italian and German air power in-theatre been brought to bear, the retreat could have ended in a rout.

The Allies halted their retreat at El Alamein, which had been previously chosen as 'the best place for a final resistance' against an advancing Axis army. The great El Qattara depression, which was practically impenetrable to motorised forces, rendered Rommel's famous pincer strategy impossible – he had used this tactic with great success up to that point in the desert campaign. Moreover, the line had been well fortified with fresh reserve troops, obstacles and minefields.

Finally, and most importantly, during the course of 1942 full co-operation between the 8th Army and the Desert Air Force had been

C.202s of 3° and 4° *Stormi* sit at Castelbenito awaiting their next sortie in early 1943. The fighter in the foreground was the aircraft assigned to 97ª *Squadriglia* commander, Capitano Fernando Malvezzi, who was credited with ten kills

attained. Such co-operation did not just happen overnight, having instead been tried and tested throughout the various advances and retreats that had punctuated the North African campaign to date. Such a system was totally lacking amongst the Italian forces, which meant that the *Regia Aeronautica* could not guarantee functional tactical support for Axis troops on the ground. This failure would soon prove fatal.

5ª *Squadra Aerea* committed its entire available force in support of Rommel's three-pronged attack on the defensive line at El Alamein on 31 August. At this time Italian aircraft had a declared average service-ability rate of just 60 per cent, which compared with the RAF figure of between 73 and 77 per cent. The African desert was an operational theatre which tested aircraft to their limits. Sand found its way into everything, and when mixed with engine oil it produced a ruinous abrasive 'sludge'. Air filters for Italian fighters were only made available late on in the campaign, reflecting the fact that senior officers in the *Regia Aeronautica* felt that problems could be solved through impulse and improvisation, rather than through effective logistical attention! Finally, the many different types, and models, of fighter in use by the *Regia Aeronautica* come late 1942 created its own maintenance problems, for spare parts were never available in abundance.

At El Alamein, a total of 600 to 700 Italian and German aircraft went into action against a force numbering in excess of 1000 fighters and bombers. And of the 700 aircraft available to the Axis, only 150 were fighters and 180 dive-bombers and fighter-bombers, the remainder being transports and reconnaissance types.

On the ground, overall control of the 8th Army had passed to General Bernard Montgomery, who was a firm believer in co-operation between air and ground forces.

Notwithstanding the courage displayed by all Axis soldiers and airmen involved in Rommel's daring assault, his attack on El Alamein failed completely. The Desert Air Force had countered with a savage campaign aimed at knocking out armoured units in the frontline, and by the time the second Battle of El Alamein was launched by the Allies on 23 October 1942, the fortunes of war in North Africa had swung against the Axis forces for the final time.

As soon as Rommel's campaign had commenced, logistical problems arose due to his army's long line of supply which extended as far back as the main port of Tripoli. On the other hand, the British could count on being resupplied by well-equipped bases in Egypt, which meant that an Allied tank could cover the distance from Port Said to the frontline at El Alamein in a day. It would take three days for an Italian or German tank to reach Benghasi from Tobruk, and longer if it had to come from Tripoli.

Montgomery's offensive, which started with a fierce artillery barrage on 23 October, had its decisive moments on 31 October and

1 November. At that time, whilst Australian troops engaged German forces, British units penetrated the Axis front to the south. On 2 November Rommel informed Hitler of his decision to retreat.

Plans to halt the retreat at Fuka and Marsa Matruh were hastily abandoned, troops instead falling back to the old borders. By this stage the Desert Air Force had achieved air superiority over the frontline, their cause being aided by the introduction of mobile radar sites which rapidly detected approaching Axis aircraft. On 12 November the last of Rommel's troops left Egypt, and the following day Tobruk fell.

Meanwhile, on 8 November a formidable Anglo-American force had invaded the Vichy French colonies in North Africa as part of Operation *Torch*. Rommel immediately understood that his forces in North Africa now had no hope of survival, for the enemy had effectively surrounded the Axis strongholds in western Libya and Tunisia.

Italian and German troops rapidly fell back on Tripoli, and then Tunisia. Such a move made perfect sense, for Tunisia was the closest point to the African continent from Sicily, and boasted terrain that was ideally suited for a 'last ditch' defence with only modest forces. Italian and German air units immediately went on the offensive in opposition to the *Torch* landings, but their efforts remained largely uncoordinated.

In a typical example of the haphazard approach to combating the Allied assault, ten S.84s bombers of 32º *Stormo* left Sardinia to attack the port of Bona, expecting to rendezvous with a fighter escort of 12 C.202s en route. The bombers arrived late at their meeting point due to adverse weather, and devoid of radio equipment, they were forced to perform the raid without escort, loosing three of their number to fighters. Three more S.84s were destroyed on landing, while the other four all returned heavily damaged, with dead and wounded on board.

Units continued to perform as best they could in-theatre, although lacking such basic items as field lights for night-time operations meant that they achieved very little. The continuous reinforcement of USAAF and RAF units in North Africa only served to exacerbate the problems facing Axis forces in their efforts to counter *Torch*, and heavy losses were duly inflicted on both fighter and bomber units.

During the final phase of the offensive at Medenine in March 1943, all Italian fighters, along with their German counterparts, were committed in one last desperate battle in the face of overwhelming odds (calculated to be around six-to-one). Their efforts were hardly felt by the Desert Air Force, whose bombers hit all Axis fighter airfields. By mid-April only the remnants of 54º *Stormo* remained in Tunisia.

On 6 May Anglo-American forces stormed the last Axis positions, this assault being preceded by a series of co-ordinated bombing missions. The following day Allied forces marched into Tunisia and Bizerta, and on 13 May Axis forces surrendered. The Allies were now ready to launch their assault on Italy and the rest of southern Europe.

MALTA

Upon the declaration of war, few Italians genuinely believed that the twin islands of Malta could adequately defend themselves against the might of the *Regia Aeronautica* based on nearby Sicily. Sensing a quick victory, it was Mussolini himself who ordered 2ª *Squadra Aerea* to immediately commence raids on the tiny British-held islands. On the morning of 11 June 1940 33 S.79s, escorted by 18 fighters, attacked Valletta harbour.

It is well known that at that time Malta's aerial defences consisted of just four Sea Gladiators,

but on 21 June eight Hurricanes had been flown in via France. The *Regia Aeronautica* soon felt the repercussions of their arrival, with aircraft being lost to the Hawker fighters throughout July.

Comiso-based CR.42s of 23º *Gruppo* (under the command of Maggiore Tito Falconi) were initially entrusted with escorting the S.79s sent to attack Malta, and the Fiat fighter was soon found wanting when it attempted to stave off the attacking Hurricanes.

And it was not just Malta's brave and capable defenders who created problems for the Italian air force between September and December 1940. Fighting on the Balkan, Libyan and Aegean fronts all absorbed precious forces from 2ª *Squadra Aerea*, whose already modest means were over-stretched and widely dispersed. Many units that had been detached to Sicily in order to sustain the attacks on Malta were posted to other theatres, and by the end of 1940 only 1º *Stormo* remained.

The spring of 1941 saw the Italians commence a new campaign to knock out the strategically-important Mediterranean islands, 7º *Gruppo* transferring to Ciampino for operations against Malta in May. The following month it was joined by 16º *Gruppo*, and control of both units passed to 54º *Stormo*, which had been transferred in to replace 1º *Stormo* after the latter outfit had been ordered to return to Campoformido, north-east of Venice.

In October the C.202 made its combat debut over Maltese skies with 4º *Stormo's* 9º *Gruppo*, the new fighter replacing the older C.200s of 54º *Stormo* – more C.202s of 51º *Stormo's* 155º and 20º *Gruppi* duly arrived in May and June 1942, respectively. During this period the Reggiane Re.2001 also entered service when 18 examples were flown into San Pietro di Caltagirone by 2º *Gruppo Autonomo*.

Practically all fighter units within the *Regia Aeronautica* would see action over Malta at one time or another up until late October 1942, when the Italians abandoned any hope of neutralising the Allied stronghold.

RUSSIAN CAMPAIGN

When German troops launched their surprise invasion of the Soviet Union on 22 June 1941, they had first passed through numerous friendly states such as

One unit that found itself heavily involved in the Malta campaign was 54° *Stormo*, which was primarily equipped with C.200s through to the end of 1942. These three Macchi fighters – from 7° *Gruppo* – were photographed in front of Pantelleria's distinctive rock-hewn hangars during late 1941. '86-8', '98-2' and '98-7' were built by Aermacchi, SAI Ambrosini and Breda respectively

Another protagonist involved in the Malta campaign was 4° *Stormo*, which flew some of the first combat sorties with the C.202 in late September 1941. Amongst the initial batch of Macchi fighters issued to the *stormo* was this aircraft (MM 7735 '97-5'), which was taken on charge by 9° *Gruppo's* 97ª *Squadriglia*. Five-kill ace Sottotenente Iacopo Frigerio scored his first victory with the C.202 whilst flying the near-identically marked '97-2' on 30 September 1941

Finland, Rumania and Hungary – all of whom immediately declared war on the USSR. Italy also followed suit, although its contribution to the fighting in the east would prove to be rather modest.

On 30 June Mussolini offered Hitler an armed corps, which was constituted on 10 July as the *Corpo di Spedizione in Russia* (CSIR – Expeditionary Corps in Russia). Its air arm was organised on 30 July under the joint command of 22° *Gruppo Caccia* and 61° *Gruppo Osservazione Aerea*. The fighter element, which had flown in to

Tudora (just north of the Rumanian border) from Tirana, consisted of 51 C.200s distributed among 359ª, 362ª, 369ª and 371ª *Squadriglie*. They were quickly sent further north to the small airfield of Krivoi-Rog, just south of the River Dnieper. With the Axis forces driving deep into the USSR, the C.200s followed the advance to Saporoshje, east of the Dnieper, in late October.

The fighters typically flew in support of ground divisions throughout the *gruppo's* time in the east, although they also occasionally escorted reconnaissance aircraft and German bombers. At first, clashes with Soviet aircraft presented few problems, as the most common fighter encountered was the small, obsolescent Polikarpov I-16 – a type thoroughly familiar to the Italian veterans of the Spanish Civil War.

However, the Soviets soon started fielding better fighters in increasing numbers, although the worst enemy facing Axis forces was the notoriously bleak Russian winter. Engines had to be pre-heated before they could be started in order to thaw out oil and hydraulic fluid. Despite such conditions, operations continued up to 31 December, by which time 12 enemy fighters and bombers had been shot down.

The extreme conditions of the Russian winter slowed up all air activity, and it was not until 5 February 1942 that the Macchis returned to action when they strafed the airfield of Krasnjy Liman. Other aerial engagements took place on the 24th and 28th of that month when four I-16s were credited to the C.200s of the 22° *Gruppo*.

Following the long winter lull, it was decided to reinforce the Italian contingent in Russia in the hope of an eventful summer. An *Armata Italiana in Russia* (ARMIR – Italian Army in Russia) was duly created, and the air element was enlarged and renamed *Comando Aeronautica Fronte Orientale* (CAFO). In May an exhausted 22° *Gruppo* was replaced by 21° *Gruppo* (356ª, 382ª and 386ª *Squadriglie*), the latter outfit also incorporating a fourth *squadriglia* (C.200-equipped 361ª).

With the renewed Axis offensive in the late spring of 1942, the Italian fighter force moved further east into the USSR, operating firstly from Stalino (to where 21° *Gruppo* had initially moved upon its arrival in-theatre) and then Voroscilovgrad, just south of the River Donetz. Using the latter airfield as its main base, the *gruppo* sent flights of

Another pilot to enjoy success at the controls of the C.202 over Malta was 360ª *Squadriglia's* Maresciallo Pasquale Bartolucci, who is seen here posing in front of his Macchi fighter. Part of 51° *Stormo's* 155° *Gruppo*, this unit was committed to the campaign between June and October 1942, when the Axis offensive petered out. Note that ten small mice have been added below the unit emblem (which normally featured a black cat catching three green rodents). These additional mice represented victories scored by the *squadriglia* over Malta up to that point in the campaign. Bartolucci ended the war with four personal and two shared victories

Like most aircraft committed to the conflict on the Eastern Front, the C.200 proved totally unsuited to operations in the freezing temperatures of the Russian winter. With its cowling covered in a canvas 'blanket', and hot air being piped directly onto the frozen engine through lengths of ducting, this Macchi fighter is being 'thawed out' in preparation for a rare winter sortie. One can only imagine how many layers of clothing the poor pilot must have donned prior to flight, for he was sat in an open cockpit! This aircraft belongs to 22° *Gruppo Autonomo*, whose distinctive 'scarecrow' emblem can be clearly seen beneath the cockpit

Seen at Saporoshje in the autumn of 1941, this 22° *Gruppo* C.200 wears typical Eastern Front markings – yellow fuselage band, nose and wingtip undersides, together with white triangles on wing leading edges. This aircraft was often flown by the CO of 369ª *Squadriglia*, Capitano Giovanni Cervellin, who claimed 13 shared victories in Russia

Macchis further forward to bases just behind the frontline as and when they were needed.

In September 12 C.202s (followed later by two photo-reconnaissance variants) were flown into Stalino in an effort to counter the improved quality of opposing aircraft, and the increasing obsolescence of the C.200s. Bad weather hampered the mission effectiveness of the new fighters, however, and they managed only 17 sorties in total. They failed to shoot down a single aircraft, but equally did not suffer any losses.

After months of retreating eastwards, the Soviets unleashed a massive counter-offensive in December which routed both the German 6th and Italian 8th Armies. Lacking a secure airfield from which to fly from, totally outnumbered in the air and suffering poor serviceability with their worn out C.200s, 21° *Gruppo* completed its last operation on 17 January 1943. Five days later it was pulled back to Stalino, where it abandoned 15 unserviceable Macchis and headed for home.

DEFENCE OF SICILY AND ITALY

During the Casablanca Conference (codenamed *Symbol*) held in January 1943 between President Roosevelt and Prime Minister Churchill, and their respective Chiefs of Staff, the decision was taken to attack Sicily once Axis forces had been expelled from North Africa. The plan was worked out in greater detail during the Trident Conference held in Washington in May, when Churchill, in particular, pushed for the invasion of Italy in an effort to relieve the pressure being exerted on Soviet forces on the Eastern Front.

Sicily was seen as the first step in this campaign, although the tiny island of Pantelleria, midway between Tunisia and Sicily, had to be neutralised first. Small but strategically important, Pantellaria, together with Lampedusa, provided Italian and German forces with defensive 'eyes' in this region thanks to the radar installations positioned on both islands.

A *squadriglia* of C.202s from 151° *Gruppo* provided the direct defence of Pantelleria, together with a flight of CR.42 nightfighters. Lacking sufficient underground shelters for all the aircraft on the island, continual bombing raids, and shelling from allied warships offshore, caused such damage to the airfield that the *Regia Aeronautica* decided to evacuate virtually the whole *gruppo* to Sicily on 21 May.

The 115-kill German ace Oberst Werner Mölders is briefed on the C.200 during a visit to 22° *Gruppo* soon after the unit's arrival on the Eastern Front in August 1941

The C.202 was not committed to the Eastern Front until September 1942, when 12 Breda-built examples were divided evenly between each of 21° *Gruppo's* three *squadriglie*. This particular Macchi fighter was assigned to 382ª *Squadriglia*, commanded by Capitano Enrico Candio (who claimed one personal and three shared victories)

With just four C.202s left behind to defend Pantelleria, surrender was inevitable, and on 11 June the Allies seized the island. During the final 11 days of fighting in defence of Pantelleria, only 250 Axis aircraft had managed to get airborne, of which 57 were shot down. Conversely, Anglo-American forces had lost 43 aircraft during the brief campaign.

With a formidable armada at their disposal, the Allies made preparations for the invasion of Sicily and, if all proceeded as planned, the conquest of the southern flank of 'Fortress Europe'. At the same time Italy prepared for the defence of Sicily, and on the eve of the invasion, the *Regia Aeronautica* could count on 359 airworthy aircraft in the following units – 4° *Stormo*, with its 48 C.202s and C.205Vs of 9° and 10° *Gruppi* dispersed between Catania and Gerbini, and their satellite airstrips, 21° *Gruppo* with 12 C.202s at Chinisia, 3° *Gruppo* with 17 Bf 109Gs at Comiso, 150° *Gruppo* with 25 Bf 109s at Sciacca, and a flight of seven C.202s from 153° *Gruppo* charged with defending Palermo itself.

Also at readiness were 60 fighter aircraft in central Italy, based halfway between Sardinia and Sicily at Ciampino-Roma, which could provide immediate defensive or offensive support to Sicilian units. These took the form of 3° and 51° *Stormi*, controlling 22°, 160° and 24° *Gruppi* equipped with C.202s, C.205Vs, Re.2001s and Re.2005s. Other autonomous bomber, ground attack, dive-bomber and fighter units were dispersed at bases in Sardinia, Calabria, Puglia and Campania, and these would also available to provide support wherever possible.

The Luftwaffe's *Luftflotte 2* was similarly prepared, having at its disposal an intervention force of five fighter, four ground attack and six bomber *gruppen*, dispersed in Sicily, Sardinia, Puglia, Calabria and Campania. This force amounted to 350-400 aircraft.

The Axis plan, although theoretically sound, was thrown into disarray by overwhelming Allied air power. Bombers hammered eastern and western airfields in Sicily for ten days and nights without respite, rendering them practically unusable. These strikes forced the withdrawal of the shattered fighter units from the western and central bases on the island, leaving the remnants concentrated on the plains near Catania. The Allies then went after these aircraft, and on 5 July alone, 104 fighters were destroyed at Catania and Gerbini in raids that saw 1400 tons of bombs dropped. Two days later, Allied reconnaissance confirmed the presence on eastern airfields of 71 Italian and 179 German fighters, together with eight bombers. These were quickly destroyed in follow-up raids.

By 9 July the *Regia Aeronautica* had lost 220 aircraft on Sicilian airfields and 53 in aerial combat – the Germans had lost a further 93 fighters. 3º and 150º *Gruppi* had been practically wiped out when their advanced bases on the western coast, at Sciacca and Comiso,

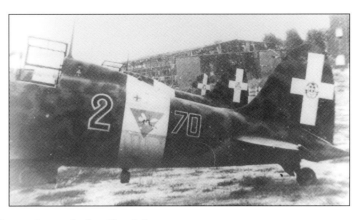

were hit, although 4º *Stormo* and 21º *Gruppo* had suffered fewer casualties. The massive bombing raid on Sciacca of 11 July destroyed nearly all the Italian Bf 109Gs on the island, and killed 344 men.

During the opening phase of the Sicilian invasion in the early hours of 10 July, the airports at Gela and Pachino had been swiftly captured, cleared of mines and their runways re-levelled to allow Spitfires and Warhawks to be flown in from Malta. The first concrete reaction by the *Regia Aeronautica* to these landings took place at dawn on the 10th, when 13 Z.1007s took off from Perugia to attack ships and landing craft. Although they managed to hit some of their targets, four aircraft were lost in the process. Other raids by Axis aircraft followed, and the Allies registered their first losses of naval and landing craft. On that day, no less than 500 sorties were mounted to counter the invasion.

In Italy, the *Regia Aeronautica's* invasion plans came into effect, with eight Re.2005s of 22º *Gruppo* scrambling from Naples, eight C.202s of 3º *Stormo* departing Cerveteri, ten C.205s of 51º *Stormo* leaving Capoterra and Monserrato and 14 Ju 87s of 103º *Gruppo Tuffatori* heading for Sicily from Decimo. Other aircraft sent into action included 15 CR.42s of 15º *Stormo Assalto* from Oristano, 32 Re.2002s of 5º *Stormo* from Tarquinia, 45 G.50s of 158º and 159º *Gruppo Assalto* from Pistoia, 14 Ju 87s of 121º *Gruppo* from Siena and 11 S.84s from Lonate Pozzolo.

About 160 Italian aircraft were lost in the first days after the invasion, 57 of which fell between 10 and 12 July alone – most were claimed by Anglo-American fighters and anti-aircraft fire. Those aircraft that managed to survive their combat missions were subsequently destroyed on the airfields at Catania, Gerbini, Reggio Calabria, Crotone, Grottaglie and Palermo. On the 16th, Sicilian air command ordered the evacuation back to Italy of all units at airfields in Calabria and Puglia, and five days later it too pulled back to the mainland.

Just a dozen C.202s from 155º *Gruppo* and a similar number of CR.42s from 46º *Gruppo Assalto*, together with a handful of German fighters, remained scattered between the airfields at Catania and Gerbini. These aircraft rarely ventured aloft in the final weeks of the defence of Sicily, the island falling into Allied hands on 17 August following the departure of the remaining Italian and German defenders.

During July and August fighter units of the *Regia Aeronautica* performed 1152 sorties in the ill-fated defence of Sicily. Such strenuous

Three C.202s of 70ª *Squadriglia* (23º *Gruppo*, 3º *Stormo*) sit outside the bomb-ravaged hangars at Cerveteri, north of Rome, in August 1943. Superimposed on the white rudder cross is the emblem of the Italian State without the fasces, this important change to the House of Savoy's coat of arms being introduced following the fall of Mussolini's fascist government on 25 July 1943. 3º *Stormo* was entrusted with the defence of central Italian skies during the summer of 1943, and among its more successful pilots were Sergente Maggiore Gorrini and Tenente Bordoni Bisleri

activity took a heavy toll in both men and machinery, and by the time the island fell, the Allies had achieved total air supremacy.

Allied airpower now switched its focus to targets on the Italian mainland. Between the spring of 1943 and 8 September, towns and cities were subjected to a series of carpet bombing raids in an attempt to break public morale as a prelude to a final collapse. Among the primary targets were Turin, Milan, Genoa, La Spezia and Naples. Still reeling from the slaughter over Sicily, emasculated fighter units coped as best they could with the situation, downing a good number of Allied aircraft – pilots were credited with more than 275 victories.

This tally shows how quickly Italian pilots adapted their tactics to counter the massive formations of B-17s and B-24s that were now appearing over their homeland. Learning from the experiences of their German allies, creditable results were attained by outstanding pilots such as Tenente Bordoni Bisleri and Sergente Maggiore Gorrini.

However, such actions all ultimately proved to be in vain, for the invasion of Sicily and the Allied bombardment of Rome had finally resulted in the dismissal of Benito Mussolini and the dissolution of the Fascist Party by the restored Italian monarch, King Victor Emmanuel III, on 25 July. On 3 September the new government, led by Marshal Pietre Badoglio, signed an armistice agreement with the Allies, which was made public five days later. That same day the Allied armies invaded the mainland. Italy was now effectively split in two, with the Germans and Italian Fascists fighting on in the north of the country.

TWO AIR FORCES

Mirroring the split in Italy in the wake of the Armistice, the air force also broke up into two factions which, in many respects, were very similar. Indeed, it often appeared as if they were only divided by the insignia they carried on their respective aircraft – the pre-Fascist roundel in the south and the Italian flag, with fasces, in the north.

The men on either sides drew their heritage from a common history which bred the same heroes – both air forces, for example, named units after leading World War 1 ace Francesco Baracca! And as in the days of the *Regia Aeronautica*, pilots and groundcrews struggled on with poor equipment and little logistical support.

At the time of the Armistice, the majority of what remained of the *Regia Aeronautica* was based in the central and northern regions of the Italian peninsular, where it had gradually retreated under the constant pressure of Anglo-American air power. With the announcement of the Armistice, such geographical locations facilitated the capture of many aircraft by the Germans. With a substantial number of units in the south now lacking any equipment, most opted simply to disband.

One of the new fighter types issued to the *Regia Aeronautica* in the final months of its existence was the Macchi C.205V, which immediately won favour with Italian pilots. This particular example was from the first production series, which entered service lacking the 20 mm Mauser cannon armament. Assigned to 360ª *Squadriglia* (155° *Gruppo*, 51° *Stormo*), this aircraft was committed to the ill-fated defence of Sardinia in the summer of 1943

In the north, an agreement was reached in October between the *Sottosegretario all'Aviazione* (Undersercretary for Aviation), Tenente Colonello Ernesto Botto, and the Luftwaffe commander in Italy (*Luftflotte 2*), Generalfeldmarschall Wolfram von Richthofen, for the creation of a temporary air force nucleus. With Tenente Colonello Giuseppe Baylon chosen as deputy head of the air ministry, Botto gave the new air force the name *Aeronautica Repubblicana* (Republican Air Force), to which was added the word *Nazionale* (National) in June 1944.

A 22° *Gruppo Autonomo* C.202 flies past one of Italy's symbolic landmarks, Mount Vesuvius, just south of Naples. This unit was based at nearby Napoli-Capodichino during the defence of southern Italy, and suffered terrible losses attempting to defend the port city from Allied heavy bombers

Paramount among the many problems facing the new air arm was a solution to the difficult relationship the Italian forces now had with their German allies, who viewed them solely as a subordinate partner for the provision of labour and resources. As an example of this mentality, while the *Aeronautica Repubblicana* was struggling to form and equip its own autonomous units, the Germans requisitioned over 1000 aircraft of all types. This situation was only solved towards the end of 1943 when a number of C.205Vs were handed back by JG 77 to enable the formation of Iº *Gruppo Caccia*, which made its combat debut over Turin on 3 January 1944.

Point defence became the primary mission of the *Aeronautica Repubblicana*, with the next unit to be formed being *Squadriglia Complementare 'Montefusco'*, equipped with G.55s, followed by IIº *Gruppo Caccia* in April. When supplies of Italian-built fighters began to run out, these units began to convert onto Bf 109Gs handed over by JGs 53 and 77 in mid 1944. Just prior to this, at the end of April, Iº *Gruppo* had been transferred from Campoformido to Reggio Emilia – it moved again, at the end of June, to Thiene (Vicenza). By then IIº *Gruppo* had also shifted from Bresso (Milan) to Bologna, before transferring to Aviano for conversion training onto the Bf 109. It was then sent to the new base at Villafranca.

In early 1944 the *Aeronautica Nazionle Repubblicana* (ANR) commenced its defence of northern Italy, and one of its principal weapons was the C.205V. This cannon-armed third series aircraft was assigned to Iº *Gruppo Caccia's* 1ª *Squadriglia*, being flown by the unit's CO, Capitano Adriano Visconti

Apart from suffering high losses in the face of overwhelming opposition, Italian morale was further eroded by the German reluctance to replenish the units with much needed aircraft. Indeed, the Luftwaffe high command constantly pushed for the absorption of the entire ANR within its own ranks on the Italian front. It even went as far as to attempt such an objective through the formation of the *Legione Aerea Italiana* in late August 1944, but this only succeeded in bring a total halt to all ANR activity for nearly three months.

With all Luftwaffe fighter assets now pulled back from Italy to help in the defence of Germany, IIº *Gruppo* at last resumed operations in November. The following month Iº *Gruppo* was transferred to Germany to undergo conversion training onto the Bf 109G, and it returned to Italy just in time to participate in the final days of the conflict. Despite the futility of intercepting vast numbers of Allied aircraft, Iº *Gruppo* nevertheless engaged the enemy, and paid a high price in terms of both aircraft and men lost.

2 April 1945 marked the blackest day in the brief annals of IIº *Gruppo*. Twenty-four Bf 109s took off from Aviano and Osoppo, and although three turned back due to technical problems, the rest flew towards Lake Garda and thence to Ghedi (Brescia). There, they intercepted a large formation of B-25s, escorted by P-47Ds of the 347th Fighter Squadron. In the one-sided battle that ensued, the Italian pilots suffered a catastrophic defeat, losing no fewer than 14 Bf 109s and six pilots killed without scoring a single victory.

The last fighter missions flown by the ANR took place on 19 April, and involved both *gruppi*. Pilots of Iº *Gruppo* claimed a B-24 destroyed, while their counterparts in IIº *Gruppo*, which sortied its entire complement of 26 Bf 109s in an attempt to intercept a forma-

tion of Mitchells, were jumped by escorting P-51Ds and lost five aircraft without ever getting close to the medium bombers.

Having defended the skies of Italy up to the very end of the war, Maggiore Adriano Visconti, CO of Iº *Gruppo* (and a notable fighter ace), negotiated the surrender of his unit, with full military honours, with local Italian partisans. A few hours later he was killed in the court-yard of a Milan barracks, shot in the back by an unknown partisan, together with his flight adjutant, Sottotenente Stefanini.

—— AIR FORCE IN THE SOUTH ——

Following the declaration of war against Germany of 13 October 1943, the Italian government in the south was accorded Co-Belligerant, but not full ally, status. As with the *Aeronautica Repubblicana*, the *Aeronautica Co-Belligerante* (Co-Belligerant Air Force) was blighted by a serious shortage of aircraft, spares, replacement pilots, fuel and even accommodation.

Of all the units based in the central sector of Italy at the time of the Armistice, only 8º *Gruppo* moved south in its entirety to the demilitarised zone as instructed in the agreement signed between the Allies and Marshal Badoglio's government. Initially transferred to Tunisia, it finally re-entered Italy, equipped with its worn-out C.200s, under the leadership of Maggiore Mario Bacich in the late autumn of 1943.

Many other units such as 4º, 5º and 51º *Stormi* were already in the zone when the Armistice was announced, having been based in Calabria and Sardinia up until late August. Other aircraft reached southern bases from all over Italy, some units having had to fight their way out of bases in the north.

Faced with a shortage of resources, and cut off from Italy's aviation industry (all major production facilities were in the north of the country), the task of forming a small, but efficient air force, proved to be no mean feat. This was made all the more difficult when the few serviceable airfields and aviation-related industrial centres in the south were requisitioned by the Allies for their own needs – the Alfa Romeo plant at Pomigliano d'Arco, for example, was taken over for the servicing of British transport vehicles.

Eleven-kill ace Maresciallo Magnaghi obtained eight of his victories over Malta. He is seen posing alongside a C.205V of Iº *Gruppo Caccia* just prior to his death in action on 13 May 1944

This G.55 was flown by the *Squadriglia Complementare Montefusco-Bonet*, based at Venaria Reale, in April 1944. The fighter carries its namesake's signature just aft of the propeller, Bonet having been killed in action just moments after he shot down his last four-engined bomber (a B-17 from the 2nd BG) on 29 March 1944. Bonet's Fiat fighter was claimed by 18-kill ace Herschel 'Herky' Green, who was flying a 317th FS/325th FG P-47D at the time. Having not previously encountered the rare G.55 in combat, Green stated in his combat report that he had destroyed a 'Fw 290'

This left the *Aeronautica Co-Belligerante* with little option but to scour airfields used by the former *Regia Aeronautica* – some of which were as far away as North Africa – for useable parts that could be stripped off dumped and battle-damaged aircraft. This effort soon bore fruit, and resulted in a goodly number of C.202s being converted into C.205s through the substitution of the former's Daimler-Benz DB 601 engine with a DB 605.

All five of these pilots from Iº *Gruppo Caccia's* 1ª *Squadriglia* scored victories during the defence of Italy. They are, from left to right, Sergente Diego Rodoz (six kills), Tenente Bruno Cartosio (four kills), Tenente Vittorio Satta (two kills), Tenente Antonio Weiss (two kills) and Tenente Mario Cavatore (three kills)

When further aircraft, and parts, could no longer be found, and unserviceability began to seriously effect the operability of the *Aeronautica Co-Belligerante*, the Allies equipped six *gruppi* with Martin Baltimore medium bombers, Bell P-39 Airacobras and Supermarine Spitfire Mk Vs. The arrival of the new equipment totally reinvigorated the air arm, for Italian pilots at last realised just how wide a technological gap existed between the local aircraft industry and its counterparts in Britain and the USA.

On the operational side, the Allies wisely prohibited the *Aeronautica Co-Belligerante* from conducting operations over Italian territory. Most airfields had been requisitioned for use by Anglo-American fighter and bomber units in any case, leaving Italian pilots in the south to congregate primarily at Lecce. Smaller groups of airworthy aircraft could also be found in Sardinia, whilst the *Raggruppamento Idrovolanti* (Seaplane Group) was dispersed at moorings between Taranto and Brindisi.

With Italian airspace operationally out of bounds, the *Aeronautica Co-Belligerante* was packed off to operate from airfields located in newly-liberated areas of the Balkans. Over 500 supply sorties were subsequently flown in 1943-44, two-thirds of which were in support of Yugoslav partisans, and the rest supporting Italian troops on the grorund that had remained isolated in German-controlled areas following the Armistice.

The *Raggruppamento Caccia*, commanded by Tenente Colonnello Fanali, provided escorting fighters for the transports, and also conducted ground attack missions often at the very limits of their range. Operating from the most austere of airfields, *Aeronautica Co-Belligerante* units suffered extreme hardship, especially during the freezing winter months. The weather was not the only problem facing the air force in the final months of the war, for the Italian desire to maintain as many active units as possible, and therefore keep morale intact, at the cost of technical efficiency was in complete contrast to Allied wishes. Eventually, the rationalisation of flying equipment resulted in some cutbacks, including the forced inactivity of 9º *Gruppo* (4º *Stormo*) during the winter of 1944-45.

However, a small, but well-organised, cadre of units did survive through to VE-Day, and these went on to form the basis of the modern Italian Air Force.

MAIN FIGHTER UNITS

1º *STORMO*

This was the first autonomous fighter unit to become operational during World War 1, being redesignated a *stormo* on 7 May 1923. Its 6º *Gruppo* began World War 2 supporting the bombing campaign against Malta in the company of 17º *Gruppo*, which was originally equipped with Fiat CR.32s and, later, Macchi C.200s. After a year of operations, the *stormo* was posted to Campoformido in July 1941, where it reorganised and converted onto the Macchi C.202. On completion of its re-equipment, the unit moved to Libya.

During the initial Italo-German offensive in North Africa, the *stormo* was given the task of protecting Italian troops from attack by Allied aircraft. By the end of the campaign in July 1942, it had been credited with the destruction of 125 enemy aircraft, although heavy attrition of its own C.202s had seen the unit practically wiped out. 1º *Stormo* was then transferred to the tiny island of Pantelleria, and later to Decimomannu, in Sardinia.

During the final year of the war, clashes between the unit's C.202s and an ever increasing number of enemy aircraft became more frequent. In June 1943, following re-equipped with the Macchi C.205V, the unit completed its last operational missions escorting torpedo-bombers and defending the Sicilian Channel. By the time of the Armistice, 6º and 17º *Gruppi* were operating their few aircraft from an airstrip at Osoppo, near the Austrian border. However, they saw little action prior to the demise of the *Regia Aeronautica*.

This C.202 belonged to 1º *Stormo's* 17º *Gruppo*, the fighter being the personal mount of Capitano Pio Tomaselli. The CO of 72ª *Squadriglia*, Tomaselli claimed four kills during World War 2 to add to his two Spanish war victories

2º *STORMO*

Formed at Treviso on 25 December 1925, 2º *Stormo* consisted of two *gruppi* – 8º (92ª, 93ª and 94ª *Squadriglie*) and 13º (77ª, 78ª and 82ª *Squadriglie*), flying CR.32 and CR.42 biplanes respectively – at the start World War 2. Based in Libya at the outbreak of war, the *stormo's* serviceability rate fell so rapidly during the summer of 1940 that combat readiness was severely compromised. Upon being re-equipped with overhauled machines, 2º *Stormo* returned to operations, dispersing its aircraft on a number of airfields including Derna and Sidi Magrum. Seeing much action over the next few months, 2º

Stormo claimed a number of kills, with 13º *Gruppo's* Giulio Torresi distinguishing himself with many individual victories.

Heavily committed to the Italo-German counter-offensive of September 1940, the *stormo* was bled dry of both men and machinery. Posted back to Italy, it was assigned the role of airfield defence for a number of bases in southern Italy. Re-equipped with C.200s in February 1941, 2º *Stormo* continued to fly defensive sorties, enduring a series of transfers to different bases (Novi Ligure, Albenga, Piacenza, Orio al Serio, Jesi and Milano-Linate) over the next eight months.

The *stormo* commenced its second operational tour when it returned to Africa in November 1941, one *gruppo* of C.200s being based at Martuba, on the Libyan coast, and the second just west of El Alamein at Abu Haggag. Over the next few months of intense action, some 4800 missions were flown, amounting to nearly 9000 flying hours. One particularly notable mission took place on 14 September 1942 when 13º *Gruppo* sunk the Royal Navy destroyer HMS *Zulu* and set fire to four Motor Torpedo Boats during an attempted troop landing at Tobruk.

8º *Gruppo* returned to Italy in early December 1942, leaving just three serviceable C.200s (out of a total strength of 26) for 13º *Gruppo*. The latter unit remained in Libya with a few C.200s and C.202s until the final days of the Tunisian campaign, surviving pilots finally being sent to Metato, near Pisa, in July 1943. Here, the *gruppo* performed point defence duties using its few remaining C.200s, together with 12 Dewoitine D.520s that had been acquired from Vichy French units in southern France following the German occupation in November 1942.

3º *STORMO*

Formed in 1931, 3º *Stormo Caccia* was based at Torino Mirafiori when Italy declared war on Britain and France, the unit controlling 18º *Gruppo* (83ª, 85ª and 95ª *Squadriglie*) and 23º *Gruppo* (70ª, 74ª and 75ª *Squadriglie*). Both units were equipped with CR.42s, and these were initially involved in the defence of Milan and the Ligurian coast.

On 10 July 1940 23º *Gruppo* gained autonomy, moving to Comiso, in Sicily, in order to participate in the first offensive against British forces on Malta. During this period Capitano Mario Rigatti was decorated with the Gold Medal for Military Valour, becoming one of the few living holders of this award. 18º *Gruppo*, meanwhile, was transferred to Belgium in October 1940 to form part of 56º *Stormo*.

Bereft of any *gruppi*, 3º *Stormo* was disbanded on 20 May 1941, only to be reconstituted nearly a year later, on 15 May 1942, at Mirafiori, in north-western Italy. The new *stormo* welcomed back both 18º and 23º *Gruppi* once again, the former unit equipped with C.200s and the latter C.202s.

In July both units were transferred to North Africa, where some 50 Macchis belonging to 18º *Gruppo* were used as fighter-bombers, equipped with underwing racks capable of carrying 50-kg bombs. Thrown into action against troops and columns of mechanised transport in the El Alamein zone, and escorted by the C.202s of 23º *Gruppo*, the unit scored some notable successes. However, the numeri-

Being refuelled by hand, this C.202 was flown by Capitano Mario Pinna (five kills), CO of 75ª *Squadriglia* (23° *Gruppo*, 3° *Stormo*). It carries two victory symbols on its fin

Maggiore Luigi Filippi, commander of 3° *Stormo's* 23° *Gruppo*, receives help securing his parachute harness prior to climbing aboard his already idling C.202 at Sfax, on the east coast of Tunisia. Note the *gruppo* commander's pennant to the right of the groundcrewman climbing down from the cockpit. This photograph was taken in late January 1943, and within a month seven-victory ace Filippi was dead. However, rather than being shot down in aerial combat, he was killed by a burst of gunfire from an American infantryman while trying to flee the advancing allied forces in a staff car near Sfax on 20 February

cal superiority of the opposing forces made it increasingly difficult for the unit, and other *stormi*, to obtain convincing results.

Commanding 3° *Stormo* during this period was Tenente Colonello Tito Falconi, who was fortunate enough to be surrounded by pilots of exceptional valour, including Filippi, Solaro, Solaroli, Tugnoli, Bordoni-Bisleri and Gorrini.

By the start of the Tunisian campaign in January 1943, 18° *Gruppo* was dispersed at Medenine and Gabes, and it was from these airfields in the south of the country that the unit flew interception patrols over the Italian lines around Mareth. A final move to Sfax, on the Tunisian coast, in company with other *gruppi* came at a time when the unit could muster no more than ten serviceable aircraft out of the 65 with which its three *gruppi* were originally equipped.

In March 1943 the *stormo* returned to Italy, where it was initially based at Caselle Torinese, followed by a move to Ciampino in an effort to bolster the defence of Rome against Allied air raids. 23° *Gruppo* began exchanging its C.202s for around 15 Bf 109G-6s in early July, and the following month six C.205Vs also turned up. An identical number of Macchi fighters had also been issued to 18° *Gruppo* in late July, along with between four and six SAI S.207 lightweight fighters that were assigned to 83ª *Squadriglia* for evaluation.

Months after the Armistice, in July 1944, 3° *Stormo* was reformed as the *Stormo Baltimore*, equipped with the Martin twin-engined bomber of the same name.

4° *STORMO*

Probably the most famous unit in the Italian air force, 4° *Stormo* was formed at Campoformido on 1 June 1931. In June 1940 it controlled 9° (73ª, 96ª and 97ª *Squadriglie*) and 10° *Gruppi* (84ª, 90ª and 91ª *Squadriglie*), both of which were equipped with CR.42s. Seeing brief action over Malta, the *stormo* transferred to North Africa in mid-July.

Bomber escort, interdiction, fighter sweeps and point defence missions were all flown without respite over the next six months, proving a stern test of both men and machinery. Initially based at Berka (Benghasi) and El Adem, the *stormo* moved firstly to Derna and then El Gaza in September 1940. Upon returning home at the end of the year it received C.200s for the second time. 9° and 10° *Gruppi* had

This C.200 was flown by five-kill ace Sergente Maggiore Alessandro Bladelli of 91ª *Squadriglia*, 10° *Gruppo*, 4° *Stormo*. Although this *stormo* produced the most aces, it also suffered the highest casualty rate

The prancing horse emblem used by 9° and 10° *Gruppi* was inspired by the personal marking of Italian World War 1 'ace of aces', Maggiore Francesco Baracca. This particular example adorns a 91ª *Squadriglia* C.202, this 10° *Gruppo* unit producing such famous aces as Leonardo Ferrulli (20 kills) and Carlo Maurizio Ruspoli (10 kills)

been the first units within the *Regia Aeronautica* to be issued with the new monoplane fighter earlier in the year, but the pilots of both *gruppi* preferred their obsolete CR.42s, so the Macchis were passed on to 1° *Stormo* instead!

Completing its conversion at Gorizia, 4° *Stormo* then briefly participated in the spring 1941 invasions of Greece and Yugoslavia. 9° *Gruppo* re-equipped with C.202s (again at Gorizia) in July and went on to see action over Malta from Comiso, on Sicily's southern coast, in late September. 10° *Gruppo*, meanwhile, had been supporting the Axis bombing campaign against Malta since the middle of June, the unit losing ten of its pilots (including its commander, Tenente Colonello Romagnoli) by the end of August.

Pulled out of the frontline in December, 10° *Gruppo* returned to Gorizia and spent the next four months converting onto the C.202. After a brief two-week spell in combat back over Malta in April 1942, both 9° and 10° *Gruppi*

were sent to Tripoli to commence their second tour of duty in North Africa. Led by Tenente Colonnello François, the *stormo* saw much action over the Libyan and western Egyptian coastline from airfields at Martuba, Sidi Barrani, Fuka Nord and Sud, Abu Smeit and Benghasi.

Eventually falling back to defend Tripoli with its few remaining C.202s in December 1942, 4° *Stormo* returned to Italy the following

9° *Gruppo's* prancing horse marking was applied in the reverse colours to those used by 10° *Gruppo*. This C.202 belonged to 96ª *Squadriglia*, which was commanded by nine-kill ace Tenente Emanuele Annoni when this photograph was taken in 1942

Tenente Annoni's C.202 '96-8' MM 7742 is repaired at Comiso in November 1941 after being shot up over Malta on 14 October 1941. The fighter had been struck by cannon shells fired from the No 185 Sqn Hurricane II flown by five-kill ace Plt Off David Barnwell. The British pilot was in turn shot down and killed just moments later by further C.202s

On 19 September 1942, 150-kill ace Hans-Joachim Marseille test flew Annoni's C.202 '96-10' from Fuka. The one-off flight ended in a wheels-up landing when the German ace accidently switched the engine off!

month. Both *gruppi* received a few C.205Vs to bolster its ranks of C.202s in the spring of 1943, the *stormo* being rushed from the mainland to Sicily in June to help counter the Allied invasion of the island. Returning to Crotone (on the Italian south coast) in mid-July, the *stormo* moved once again in late August, its headquarters flight, together with 9º *Gruppo*, being based at Gioia del Colle, and 10º *Gruppo* taking over an airstrip at Castrovillari.

By this time fully equipped with C.205Vs, 4º *Stormo* was eventually absorbed into the *Raggruppamento Caccia* of the *Aeronautica Co-Belligerante*, together with the 5º and 51º *Stormi*.

6º *STORMO*

6º *Stormo* was formed on 15 January 1936, and at the beginning of World War 2, its 2º *Gruppo* was based in Puglia and 3º *Gruppo* in Sardinia. The former unit operated a mix of CR.32s and G.50s, whilst the latter flew both CR.32s and CR.42s. In September 1940 both

Weighed down by his flying gear, five-kill ace Sergente Maggiore Bladelli climbs aboard his 91ª *Squadriglia* C.200 at Catania on 22 June 1941. Bladelli's mission on this day was to escort bombers heading for Malta

C.202 '90-4' MM 7795 was the regular mount of five-kill ace Sergente Amleto Monterumici of 90ª *Squadriglia*. This exact colour scheme has been reproduced on the C.202 displayed within the Air and Space Museum in Washington DC

Pilots from 2° *Gruppo* relax with a card game alongside a Reggiane Re.2001. This unit was extremely active during the spring 1942 offensive against Malta, flying from a series of bases in Sicily. Among those pilots who distinguished themselves during this period were Tenente Giorgio Pocek (5 kills), Sottotenente Carlo Seganti (5 kills), Sottotenente Agostino Celentano (7 kills), Maresciallo Olindo Simionato (5 kills) and Sergente Maggiore Cesare Di Bert (6 kills)

This all-green Re.2001 features 2° *Gruppo's* distinctive gun-totting 'chicken' emblem on its fin

gruppi became autonomous, and for a time 2° *Gruppo* served in the Mediterranean, before being transferred to North African in December of that same year.

Operating in such a hostile environment was made all the more difficult for the unit due to the fact that its G.50s lacked sand filters, and by the time 2° *Gruppo* returned to Italy in July 1941, it was totally devoid of aircraft.

Re-equipped at Gorizia with new Reggiane Re.2001s, the *gruppo* was sent to Sicily, where it played a significant part in the Mediterranean air war, particularly against Malta. A final transfer back to the Italian mainland in the spring of 1943 was just a prelude to the dissolution of the unit, which occurred soon after the events of 8 September.

Operating in much the same theatres, 3° *Gruppo* remained in Sardinia until transferred to North Africa in July 1941. Still equipped with CR.42s, the unit saw considerable action with the biplane fighter on ground strafing, nightfighting, convoy escort and port defence sorties whilst in Libya. The *gruppo* returned home in June 1942 and re-equipped with the C.200, after which it conducted convoy escort duties from bases in southern Italy and Sicily.

2° *Gruppo's* Sottotenente Carlo Seganti (third from left) had claimed five kills (four during the Malta campaign) by the time he fell victim to ranking RAF Malta ace, Canadian George Beurling, on 12 July 1942. Also killed in this action was the *gruppo's* CO, Aldo Quarantotti

3° *Gruppo* replaced its Macchis with Bf 109G-6s at Ciampino in May 1943, and then moved to Reggio Calabria and Lecce, before returning to Sicily. Most pilots flew several missions a day during this

This C.205V 'Veltro' of 360ª *Squadriglia* (155° *Gruppo*, 51° *Stormo*) was photographed at Monserrat, in Sardinia, in March 1943. The unit commander at the time was Maggiore Duilio Fanali, a veteran pilot who had first seen action flying ground attack aircraft in the Spanish Civil War. Although not an ace, Fanali nevertheless managed to shoot down future 14-kill British ace Peter Wykeham-Barnes on 4 August 1940, the latter pilot's Gladiator being one of three No 80 Sqn biplane fighters lost on this day. Fanali was serving with CR.32-equipped 160ª *Squadriglia* (12° *Gruppo Assalto*) at the time, this unit being based at El Adem, in Libya. After the war, Fanali became head of the *Stato Maggiore dell' Aeronautica* (Italian Air Ministry)

Seven-kill ace Sergente Ferruccio Serafini also won a Gold Medal for Military Valour. Here he is seen in front of his C.205V '378-2'

period, attempting to repulse numerically superior formations of Allied aircraft. Within several weeks the unit had lost virtually all of its Messerschmitt fighters in combat, and 3° *Gruppo* retired to Italy to re-equip yet again. However, the Armistice took effect before the *gruppo* could return to the fighting.

51° *STORMO*

Formed as a tactical fighter unit on 1 October 1939 at Ciampino Sud (Rome), 51° 'black cat' *Stormo* spent the first months of the war defending both Rome and Naples with a mix of CR.32s and G.50s. This first operational cycle ended in September 1940 when 21° *Gruppo* was transferred to 52° *Stormo*.

In January 1942 51° *Stormo* reformed yet again, the Ciampino-based unit being allocated 20° (C.202s) and 155° (G.50) *Gruppi*. 300ª *Squadriglia* was also established at around this time and incorporated into the *stormo*, this specialist nightfighting unit flying a handful of Caproni Vizzola F.5s and 12 CR.42s.

51° *Stormo's* original mission was to provide defensive cover for Rome and Naples, and it remained in central Italy until May 1942, when both *gruppi* took their C.202s (155° *Gruppo* had re-equipped in March) to Sicily. The *stormo* subsequently lost many of its best pilots in action over Malta, including 151ª *Squadriglia's* commander, Furio Niclot Doglio.

155° *Gruppo* also fought in Tunisia for four weeks in November-December 1942 following the Allied landings in Algiers, the unit being based at El Alouina. It then returned briefly to Sicily, before heading back to Ciampino to rejoin 51° *Stormo*.

The operational intensity of 51° *Stormo's* war between May and December 1942 is reflected by its outstanding record during this period – 1100 operational sorties flown, 109 combat missions sustained and over 150 enemy aircraft destroyed. By May 1943 the *stormo* had been posted to Sardinia, where its *gruppi* flew a mix of C.202s and C.205Vs in the defence of the island until August 1943.

The *stormo* subsequently reformed after the Armistice at Lecce, with 20°, 21° and 155° *Gruppi* continuing to see action, but this time on the Allied side.

37

53º *STORMO*

Formed at Mirafiori (Torino) on 15 May 1936, 53º *Stormo* was in control of the CR.42-equipped 150º and 151º *Gruppi* when Italy declared war. Both units operated these biplanes over France in the final days leading up to the French surrender, before undertaking the role of fighter defence for Piemonte, Liguria and Lombardy from the airfield at Caselle. In September 1940 53º *Stormo* was transferred to North Africa, along with 157º *Gruppo*, which had operated autonomously up to that time.

On 24 February 1941 157º *Gruppo* was transferred into 52º *Stormo*, resulting in 53º *Stormo* being deactivated. It remained dormant until New Year's Day 1942, when it was reconstituted at Caselle and placed in charge of the 151º and 153º *Gruppi*, flying G.50s and C.200s respectively. For the next six months the unit was given the task of defending Turin and Milan, and then in July 1942 151º *Gruppo* moved to Araxos, in Greece. In early September 153º *Gruppo* transferred to Caltagirone, in Sicily. For a brief time it was joined on the island by 151º *Gruppo*, and both units subsequently operated their C.202s side-by-side. However, 153º *Gruppo* was duly rushed to Decimomannu and Sciacca, where they remained until July of the following year.

151º *Gruppo*, meanwhile, had operated from several bases on Sicily until ordered back to Torino Caselle (along with 153º *Gruppo*) in July 1943 to re-equip with Fiat G.55s. The *stormo* had received just one example by the time the Armistice came into effect.

54º *STORMO*

In June 1940 54º *Stormo*, which was based at Treviso, mobilised onto the airfields of Vergiate and Airasca, but was not committed into action due to the teething troubles it was experiencing with its recently-arrived C.200s. The *stormo* then consisted of two *gruppi*, namely 152º (369ª, 370ª and 371ª *Squadriglie*) and 153º (372ª, 373ª and 374ª *Squadriglie*).

54º *Stormo* was disbanded in December of 1940 prior to seeing any combat, although it was duly reformed in the spring of 1941 at Treviso and this time assigned 7º (76ª, 86ª and 98ª *Squadriglie*) and 16º (83ª, 85ª and 95ª *Squadriglie*) *Gruppi*. Both units had previously seen considerable action with other *stormo* in 1940, and now re-equipped with C.200s, they returned to combat from bases in Sicily in May-June 1941. 7º *Gruppo* flew from Catania Fontanarosa (moving to Pantelleria in July 1942) and 16º operated from Gerbini.

They remained in action over Malta until mid-1942, when 7º *Gruppo* was sent to Greece and 16º *Gruppo* to Sardinia. Both returned to Crotone in August/September, where they re-equipped with the C.202. The Allies invaded North Africa two months later, and firstly

These C.200s of 153º *Gruppo* all carry the unit's distinctive 'Asso di Bastoni' emblem aft of the white fuselage band. This *gruppo* saw plenty of action with its venerable C.200s, flying in the Balkans, over the Adriatic on convoy escort duty and in Libya. These particular Macchi fighters were part of 372ª *Squadriglia*, which swapped its C.200s for CR.42s in the spring of 1941 when the *gruppo* was performing ground attack missions in North Africa

This C.202 of 98ª *Squadriglia* (7° *Gruppo*, 54° *Stormo*) is being refuelled at the soutern Italian base of Crotone in late 1942. 7° *Gruppo* had transitioned to the new Macchi fighter at this airfield in the autumn of that year, and subsequently participated in the Tunisian campaign in 1943. Arriving in North Africa in late March, 54° *Stormo* fought to virtual extinction, being the last *Regia Aeronautica* unit to leave Tunisia on 10 May

356ª *Squadriglia* flew C.200s as part of 21° *Gruppo Autonomo* in Russia in 1942-43, this unit making a significant contribution to the *gruppo's* overall tally of 74 aerial victories. The unit emblem, carried just below the cockpit of this particular fighter, consisted of a centaur, armed with a bow and arrow. The badge bore the legend 21° *Gruppo Caccia* below the centaur

16° and then 7° *Gruppi* were ordered to Tunisia.

They became the last Italian units to leave African soil when they departed Korba, south-east of Tunis, for the Sicilian airfield of Castelvetrano on 10 May 1943. With no aircraft or pilots left by the 27th of that same month, 54° *Stormo* disbanded.

21° *GRUPPO AUTONOMO*

As previously mentioned in this chapter, 21° *Gruppo* initially transferred from 51° to the 52° *Stormo* in September 1940, and then became an autonomous unit the following month. Equipped with a mix of CR.32s and C.200s, the *gruppo* remained on fighter defence duties firstly in the vicinity of Naples and then Bari until it was transferred to Stalino, near Rostov, on the Eastern Front in May 1942.

Sent to the USSR to replace battle-weary 22° *Gruppo* at Stalingrad, the unit saw action in this theatre for exactly a year. For several months 21° *Gruppo* operated from the airport at Voroscilovgrad, providing air cover for Italian troops – especially their crossing of the River Don and subsequent approach on Stalingrad. The unit received a dozen C.202s in September, but these were used sparingly by the *gruppo* due to poor weather and unserviceablity.

The onset of winter effectively grounded the unit, which flew its last sorties on 17 January 1943 around Millerovo. Five days later the *gruppo* retired to Stalino and prepared for the journey home, leaving 15 unserviceable fighters behind.

21° *Gruppo* claimed 74 kills with the C.200 during its time on the Eastern Front, losing 15 aircraft to combat or operational accidents in return.

Once back in Italy 21° *Gruppo* re-equipped with C.202s, and following a two-month training period on the Macchi fighter, the unit was sent to Sicily in June 1943. However, by August it had returned to Gioia del Colle with only a handful of serviceable C.202s left.

22° *GRUPPO AUTONOMO*

Part of 52° *Stormo* upon the outbreak of war, this G.50-equipped *gruppo* first saw action over France and Corsica in June 1940 whilst escorting S.79 bombers. In October the unit began converting from the Fiat fighter to the C.200, and by the time it was posted to Albania in

This 21° *Gruppo* C.202 was photographed at Gorizia soon after the unit had returned from its year-long tour on the Eastern Front. The aircraft still carries the markings synonymous with the ill-fated Soviet campaign, namely a yellow nose and fuselage bands, white wing leading edge triangles and the unit badge on the fin

March of the following year, 359ª, 362ª and 369ª *Squadriglie* had all received Macchis (36 in total).

Remaining in Albania for about three months, and engaging the enemy over both Greece and Yugoslavia, the unit then became 22° *Gruppo Autonomo* in preparation for its commitment to the Italian expeditionary force sent to fight the Russians. Just prior to heading north, it was joined by 371ª *Squadriglia*, which was transferred in from 157° *Gruppo*.

Equipped with 51 C.200s and based at Krivoi Rog, south of Kiev, 22° *Gruppo* made its combat debut in-theatre on 27 August 1941. The Italian pilots immediately tasted success, claiming the destruction of six SB-2 bombers and two I-16 fighters for no losses. By November 1941 the unit was heavily involved in supporting the push on Stalingrad, and often finding the weather more of a challenge than the enemy, 22° *Gruppo* suffered greatly reduced serviceability during the bitter winter months. It struggled on come the spring thaw, supporting German bombers flying missions around the River Don region. Finally relieved by 21° *Gruppo* in May 1942, the unit claimed 14 Soviet fighters and several bombers without suffering any lossses during its time in Russia.

Leaving its C.200s in the USSR for its relief *gruppo*, the unit was sent to Ciampino and re-equipped with Re.2001s over the next two months. It then moved to Sicily in September to commence anti-maritime and fighter-bomber operations against Malta. Following a near two-month spell on Sardinia in November-December 1942, the remnants of the unit (ten aircraft) returned to Napoli-Capodichino, where they exchanged their Re.2001s for a mix of C.202s and ex-French D.520s. The prototype Re.2005 and ten pre-production examples were also issued to the unit the following May, and these were used in the defence of Rome and Naples.

21° Gruppo Autonomo was led by Maggiore Ettore Foschini (right) during its time in Russia, the Spanish war veteran adding seven victories to his single pre-war kill whilst on the Eastern Front. Note that both Foschini and the anonymous cigarette-toting pilot to his right wear *gruppo* badges on their respective flying jackets

The first Italian fighter unit to appear on the Russian Front was 22° *Gruppo Autonomo*, which arrived in-theatre in August 1941. Devoid of its pilot, this C.200 has been left to run up at Saporoshje in an effort to get it properly 'thawed out' prior to flight. Beneath its cockpit appears the distinctive 'scarecrow' emblem designed by *gruppo* ace 'Bepi' Biron, who ended the war with eight individual kills (some sources claim he scored as many as ten victories)

C.202-equipped 359ª *Squadriglia* (22° *Gruppo Autonomo*) flew anti-bomber sorties from Capodichino during the defence of Italy. Despite being totally outnumbered, a small number of pilots from this unit (including Tenente Mazzitelli, with eight victories, Sergente Maggiore Ezio Dell'Acqua with four and Capitano Monaco with three) achieved notable successes against American heavy bombers

Starting the war as part of 24° *Stormo*, G.50-equipped 361ª *Squadriglia* transferred to 154° *Gruppo* in late October 1940 and went into action on the Greek-Balkans Front. Its pilots often successfully opposed RAF Gladiators, Blenheims and Hurricanes with their G.50s, the unit's leading ace of the campaign being Tenente Livio Bassi with six individual kills. He was mortally wounded crash-landing his battle-damaged Fiat on 20 February 1941

Returning to Sicily with a small force of Re.2001s in July, 22º *Gruppo* fled back to Capodichino at month end, and by the time of the Armistice its operational strength consisted of just nine airworthy C.202s.

24º *GRUPPO AUTONOMO*

Initially part of 52º *Stormo*, and charged with defending Sardinian ports with its elderly CR.32s, 24º *Gruppo* became *autonomo* when it was transferred to the Albanian capital of Tirana in October 1940. Upon arriving at the latter site the *gruppo* was issued with G.50s, which it subsequently flew in action from various airfields across Albania. Seeing combat over Yugoslavia and Greece, the unit remained in-theatre until the Balkans had come under full Axis control.

Upon its return to Italy in June 1941, the unit became involved in the aerial defence of Puglia, with 354ª and 355ª *Squadriglie* being based at Grottaglie, 361ª at Lecce and 395ª (transferred in from 154º *Gruppo*) at Brindisi. The following month 24º *Gruppo* moved to south to Sardinia, where it flew its G.50s from Alghero and Elmas in support of S.79 and S.84 torpedo bombers patrolling the Mediterranean. The Fiat monoplane proved ill-suited to these missions due to its notoriously short range, so CR.42s were also employed on many of the longer sorties.

Still flying a mix of G.50s and CR.42s come the new year, the unit now found itself intercepting ever-larger formations of Allied aircraft. Rarely forewarned of an impending attack, the 24º *Gruppo* pilots invariably scrambled into action with the bombers directly overhead. In February the unit succeeded in downing nine aircraft from three escorted raids it intercepted, and the following month its pilots participated in

no fewer than 28 scrambles. Their most successful day came on 31 March when three B-17s were shot down and a further fifteen damaged. 24º *Gruppo* did, however, pay a high price for this success, losing no less than 18 aircraft.

Finally re-equipped with a mix of C.202s, D.520s and a handful of C.205Vs during the course of May, the *gruppo* remained on Sardinia until 27 August, when it pulled back to Metato.

150º *GRUPPO AUTONOMO*

Controlled by 53º *Stormo* at the start of the war, this CR.42-equipped unit was made autonomous on 23 October when it was posted to Valona and placed 'under the wing' of *Comando Aeronautica Albania*. Converting to the C.200 at around this time, the unit saw much action during the Greek-Albanian campaign from both Valona and Devoli. During more than a year of bitter fighting in the Balkans, the *gruppo* lost a number of its best pilots, including the commanders of 364ª and 365ª *Squadriglie*, Capitani Magaldi and Graffer.

Following the Axis victory in Greece, 150º *Gruppo* transferred to North Africa, along with 371ª *Squadriglia*, which became part of 22º *Gruppo*. At the time the former unit possessed 25 C.200s, and its duties while based at Benghasi included protecting the port city's harbour and escorting naval convoys sailing between Tripoli and Tobruk. A small number of C.202s were also issued to the *gruppo* midway through 1942. Posted back to Lecce in November, it left its few surviving C.200s in-theatre for 8º *Gruppo*.

Once in Italy, the unit began its conversion onto the Bf 109, receiving a mixed group of 49 F-4s, G-4s and G-6s. Fully equipped by April, it was then thrown into action over Sicily from Sciacca, where its contribution to the island's defence cost many lives as its pilots came under constant attack both in the air and

The C.200s of 150° *Gruppo Autonomo* were also involved in the Greek-Albanian campaign, flying initially from Valona on the southern Albanian coast, before moving to Araxos and then Atene Tatoi following Greece's capitulation. This particular fighter was assigned to 364ª *Squadriglia*, which continued to fly C.200s (along with the C.202) until it received Bf 109s in April 1943. The Macchi features the distinctive 'Gigi Tre Osei' emblem adopted by the unit following the death of Sottotenente Luigi Caneppelel. The *squadriglia* was led by 14-kill ace Mario Bellagambi for much of the war

Tenente Fausto Filippi poses in front of his Bf 109G during the defence of Sicily. He used the German fighter to score most of his eight kills whilst leading 150° *Gruppo Autonomo's* 365ª *Squadriglia* prior to the armistice. Continuing to fight on with the ANR, Filippi was shot down and killed by No 417 Sqn Spitfire VIIIs on 23 January 1945

on the ground. By the time of the invasion of the island on 3 July the *gruppo* could only muster 25 serviceable aircraft.

After claiming more than a dozen victories over Sicily during the course of the month, the unit was pulled out on 28 July and posted back to Torino Casselle. The remnants of 150° *Gruppo* were still at this northern Italian base when the Armistice was announced on 8 September.

377ª *SQUADRIGLIA AUTONOMA*

Formed as a *Sezione Sperimentale* (experimental section) within 23° *Gruppo* at Comiso in August 1941, this unit was equipped with the first Re.2000 Series I to see frontline service. The losing design in the fighter fly off of 1939 that saw the C.200 and G.50 chosen to replace the CR.32 and CR.42, the Reggiane design was nonetheless put into limited production for the *Regia Marina* as a modern catapult fighter. However, such was the *Regia Aeronautica's* need for modern fighters that most went to the land-based 377ª *Squadriglia Autonoma*.

The unit was heavily engaged in operations against Malta for much of its early career, flying from several Sicilian bases as well as Sardinia. When 23° *Gruppo* was sent to Libya in December 1941, the *squadriglia* became autonomous and remained behind in Sicily. Regularly re-equipped with updated Series III Re.2000s throughout 1942, the unit remained a permanent fixture on Sicily through to the spring of 1943. By then it had also received a number of CR.42CNs to act as nightfighters, and it was in the venerable Fiat biplane that Tenente Torchio distinguished himself in combat by claiming five kills.

When spares for the Reggiane fighters became unavailable in late 1942, 377ª was provided with a dozen C.200s. Finally, in February 1943 three C.202s were also delivered to the squadron, and these were used to shoot down three four-engined bombers in April. The following month 377ª *Squadriglia* disbanded, passing its handful of aircraft and crews to 53° *Stormo*.

410ª, 411ª, 412ª AND 413ª *SQUADRIGLIE AUTONOMA*

All four units were sent to East Africa by sea in 1938, and immediately went into action from their bases in Ethiopia and Eritrea upon Italy's declaration of war in June 1940.

Flying CR.32s (410ª and 411ª) and CR.42s (412ª and 413ª), three of these *squadriglie* had soon exhausted their complement of aircraft in action, suffering bitter losses at the hands of the South African Air Force during operations around Cheren in the spring of 1941. By June only 412ª *Squadriglia* possessed any serviceable fighters, and two CR.42s continued to fight on from Gondar until the fall of Italian East Africa in late November 1941.

The *Regia Aeronautica* lacked any specialist nightfighter units (or aircraft) when it went to war in June 1940, and hastily-modified CR.42s were thrust into the role following early allied attacks on northern Italian targets. Equipped with searchlights (seen fitted here under the fighter's port wing) and, eventually, exhaust shields, these aircraft achieved only modest success. This particular CR.42 was assigned to 167° *Gruppo Autonomo's* 300ª *Squadriglia*, the former unit being created in May 1942 to oversee the nocturnal defence of both Rome and Naples

ACES AND VICTORIES

According to the official register of the Italian Air Force, 2522 enemy aircraft were shot down between 10 June 1940 and 8 September 1943. This total includes all those aircraft destroyed by fighter, bomber and reconnaissance types, but does not include aircraft destroyed on the ground, or those attributed to anti-aircraft ground fire.

During the first phase of the war, commanders usually attributed victories collectively to all those pilots who had taken part in

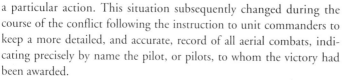

In contrast with the fighter units of other air arms involved in World War 2, those within the *Regia Aeronautica* rarely emblazoned their aircraft with kill markings. Very few exceptions have been recorded on folm, and a selection are featured on this spread. At left is the detailed silhouette of a Spitfire (complete with fuselage and underwing roundels!) that decorated the fin of an anonymous C.202 in 1942-43

Caught in the act, part one. Capitano Monaco oversees the decoration of the fin of his C.202 (from 369ª *Squadriglia*) with the planform of a B-17, having downed an American heavy bomber over southern Italy on 11 January 1943

No less than seven aircraft profiles adorn the fin of this 4° *Stormo* C.202 in North Africa. Sadly, both the pilot and the types he had shot down remain unknown

a particular action. This situation subsequently changed during the course of the conflict following the instruction to unit commanders to keep a more detailed, and accurate, record of all aerial combats, indicating precisely by name the pilot, or pilots, to whom the victory had been awarded.

However, there was still no uniform procedure in place at this time for the confirmation of aerial kills. Sometimes a third witness was deemed necessary for a victory to be credited to a pilot, whilst on other occasions only the post-sortie report from the individual directly involved in the engagement was required.

Caught in the act, part two. An airman provides the finishing touches to kill markings assigned to Sergente Maggiore Remo Broilo of 71ª *Squadriglia* (17° *Gruppo*, 1° *Stormo*). The C.202 pilot claimed two P-40 victories on 20 March 1942 whilst flying in North Africa

Caught in the act, part three. Sergente Maggiore Del Fabbro (left) and Tenente Giovanni Ambrosio, both from 378ª *Squadriglia* (155° *Gruppo*, 51° *Stormo*), decorate the fin of the latter pilot's C.202 with a Spitfire silhouette at Gela, in Sicily, soon after their epic engagement over Malta on 10 July 1942. Ambrosio, Del Fabbrio and Sergente Maggiore Francesco Visentini were credited with the destruction of two Spitfires, although RAF losses for this day reveal that only one fighter (from No 126 Sqn) failed to return to base

Finally, during March 1942, the *Stato Maggiore* was convinced of the merit of officially sanctioning and publicising individual pilot contributions. It subsequently laid down clear procedures as to how an official victory was to be confirmed.

Having failed to effectively recognise individual kills for so long, the *Regia Aeronautica* then went completely the other way during the final months of the war leading up to Armistice by offering money prizes to pilots who shot down enemy aircraft or sunk naval vessels! Unit commanders were also requested to report individual aerial victories, including those claimed in combat during previous months, in an effort to compile an accurate list. Sadly, the latter never materialised, for as with everything else in Italy, this exercise was overtaken by the 8 September 1943 announcement of the Armistice, and the immediate splitting of the air force.

Kill markings also occasionally appeared on ANR aircraft in the final months of the war, this twin-engined silhouette (perhaps signifying a B-25 or a B-26 kill) adorning the fin of this Bf 109G from II° *Gruppo Caccia*

The only officially recognised non-pilot ace of the *Regia Aeronautica* was Aviere Scelto (later Aiutante di Battaglia) Pietro Bonannini, who served as a gunner aboard Z.1007 and RS.14 reconnaissance floatplanes with 170ª *Squadriglia*, 83° *Gruppo*. Flying from Augusta floatplane base, on the east coast of Sicily, throughout the Mediterranean war, Bonannini was credited with eight aircraft shot down and two probables

In certain cases, such as those of second- and third-ranking aces Franco Lucchini and Leonardo Ferrulli, many aerial victories of the 1940-41 period were assigned collectively, which meant they remained as shared kills in official documentation.

Following the September 1942 revamping of the system set up to deal with victory accreditation, the commission responsible for the assignment of Italy's highest wartime decoration for valour, the *Medaglio d'Oro* (Gold Medal), re-examined all the combat reports from the past two years of fighting. The end result of this reappraisal was the awarding of individual kills to many of those pilots previously credited with shared victories.

In the wake of the Armistice, fighter units within the ANR adopted a kill credit system based on Luftwaffe lines, where combat reports and eyewitness accounts were closely scrutinised, along with the physical examination of any aircraft remains that were available.

Notwithstanding such stringent procedures, recent research has also established that not all aerial victories can be confirmed when counter-checked with the records of opposing forces. This comes as no great surprise, however, and only serves to confirm the general trend for fighter pilots of all air forces, under all flags, to overclaim the number of kills scored in the heat of battle.

THE ACES

We have decided that the best way to group aces within this volume is by the theatre of operation in which they claimed the most kills. Short biographies of the more notable, or high-scoring, aces make up the bulk of this chapter, the selection being limited only by available space.

Mention should also be made at this point of gunner Aviere Scelto (later Aiutante di Battaglia) Pietro Bonannini, who was almost certainly Italy's only non-pilot ace. He served in reconnaissance floatplanes (both the Cant Z.506 and Fiat RS.14), and was credited with downing eight enemy aircraft confirmed and two probables.

GREEK-ALBANIAN FRONT

Giorgio Graffer

Together with his contemporaries Mario Visintini and Luigi Baron, Capitano Giorgio Graffer was one of the first Italian pilots to obtain five aerial victories during the World War 2.

Born in Trento on 14 May 1912, Graffer was considered a brilliant student of the 'Leone' course at the *Accademia Aeronautica* (Air Force Academy). At the time of Italy's declaration of war, Graffer was in command of 365ª *Squadriglia*, 150° *Gruppo*, 53° *Stormo*, based near the French border. He performed the first night interception by a *Regia Aeronautica* pilot on 13/14 August 1940 when, flying a CR.42, he opened fire on an RAF Whitley bomber that had been sent to attack Turin. When his guns jammed, Graffer did not hesitate to ram the bomber before taking to his parachute. The aircraft had been badly damaged in the attack, and subsequently crashed into the English Channel whilst attempting to return to its base.

As a direct result of his bravery in this action, Graffer was decorated with the Bronze Medal for Military Valour. During the early stages of the invasion of Greece he shot down a further four aircraft, but was in turn killed in action over Delvinakion in a dogfight with Gladiators of No 80 Sqn on 28 November 1940. Graffer was posthumously awarded the Gold Medal for Military Valour in recognition of his heroism.

EAST AFRICA

Mario Visintini

Born at Istria on 26 April 1913, Capitano Mario Visintini became the most famous fighter pilot of the East African campaign.

On completing his higher education, he applied to enter the *Accademia Aeronautica* but failed the medical test. Undaunted, he undertook a civilian pilot course at Taliedo, near Milan, which enabled him to join the *Regia Aeronautica* as an Allievo Ufficiale Pilota di Complemento (Pilot Officer Cadet). He obtained his military 'wings' at Grottaglie in September of 1937 and was posted to 91ª *Squadriglia*, 10º *Gruppo*, 4º *Stormo* at Gorizia.

Visintini soon volunteered for service in Spain, and flying with 25ª *Squadriglia* of XVI *Gruppo 'La Cucaracha'*, he participated in a number of aerial engagements and downed an I-16 on 5 September 1938. As a result of his war record, Visintini was given a permanent commission in the *Regia Aeronautica* upon his return to Italy in November 1939.

He transferred to the CR.42-equipped 412ª *Squadriglia* in East Africa just prior to Italy's declaration of war, this unit boasting a good number of ex-4º *Stormo* pilots. Four days after Italy had entered the war on 10 June, RAF units commenced bombing missions on targets in Eritrea, and Visintini succeeded in shooting down a No 14 Sqn Vickers Wellesley (K7743, piloted by Plt Off Plunkett). He claimed a second on 3 July (L2652, flown by Flg Off S G Soderholm).

Unfortunately, in the final days prior to the Italian capitulation in East Africa, 412ª *Squadriglia*'s records were lost, making it extremely difficult to reconstruct all 16 victories attributed to Visintini during the campaign. He is known to have shot down at least five Blenheims, several more Wellesleys and almost certainly three Gladiators. He scored further successes during strafing attacks on airfields at Ghedaref,

Tenente Mario Visintini was the first Italian fighter pilot of World War 2 to earn notoriety as an 'ace', his achievements in East Africa with the CR.42 being widely publicised back in Italy. Indeed, he was so successful in aerial combat that he was dubbed 'cacciatore scientifico' ('scientific fighter pilot') by the Italian press

Tenente Visintini poses with fellow 412ª *Squadriglia* pilots in front of a suitably-marked CR.42 at Barentu, in Eritrea, in late 1940. They are, from left to, Tenente Cacciavillani, Tenente Visintini, Sottotenente D'Addetta, Tenente Di Pauli, Capitano Raffi and Sottotenente Levi. The *squadriglia* emblem featured a red prancing horse superimposed on a map of Africa, this motif bearing a strong resemblance to the 4º *Stormo* icon – many 412ª *Squadriglia* pilots had previously served with this unit

Like Visintini, fellow 412ª *Squadriglia* ace Maresciallo Aroldo Soffritti hailed from 4° *Stormo*. Credited with eight victories, five probables and eleven aircraft destroyed on the ground between 2 February and 4 April 1941, Soffritti was captured when the Italian stronghold of Dessie, in Abyssinia, fell to South African troops on 26 April 1941

Gaz Regeb and Agordat, and according to British sources these raids cost the RAF and SAAF 'tens of aircraft destroyed on the ground'.

During the attack on Gaz Regeb on 12 December 1940, the CR.42 flown by 412ª *Squadriglia* commander, Capitano Raffi, was hit by anti-aircraft fire, and he was forced to effect an emergency landing behind enemy lines. Visintini landed close to the crash site, ditched his parachute and helped Raffi aboard. He subsequently flew back to base sitting on his CO's lap!

Promoted to Capitano thanks to his operational record, and having been decorated with Silver and Bronze Medals for Military Valour, Visintini finally lost his life when his CR.42 crashed into the side of Mount Nefasit, in Eritrea, in bad weather on 11 February 1941. He was searching for his faithful wingman, Sergente Baron, at the time, that latter pilot having himself been briefly forced down by the same weather that had played such a telling part in the ace's demise.

In honour of his heroic conduct throughout the campaign, Mario Visintini was posthumously awarded the Gold Medal for Military Valour. His early demise, his undeniable success and the national fascination surrounding the fighting in the 'far-flung corners' of the Italian Empire were all elements which had made Visintini a legend in his own time. Indeed, one of the volumes of *Eroi e Avventure della Nostra Guerra* (*Heroes and Adventures of Our War*) published in 1942 was dedicated to him, being titled *Il Pilota Solitario* (*The Lonely Pilot*). His brother Licio, an officer of the *Regia Marina* (Royal Navy), was to also lose his life in action during a 'human torpedo' attack on warships in Gibraltar harbour on 8 December 1942. And like Mario, he too was posthumously awarded the Gold Medal for Military Valour.

The campaign in East Africa produced other aces apart from Visintini, namely Luigi Baron (12 and 2 shared), Aroldo Soffritti (8), Carlo Canella (7), Alberto Veronese (6 and 2 shared), Antonio Giardinà (5 and 3 shared) and Enzo Omiccioli (5).

NORTH AFRICA

Teresio Martinoli

Teresio Vittorio Martinoli, who was born at Novara on 26 March 1917, showed an intense passion for flying from an early age. He gained his glider pilots' licence in 1937, and the following year he progressed to flight training on powered aircraft to 'wings' standard. Thus qualified, Martinoli was drafted into the *Regia Aeronautica* when Italy mobilised its forces, and he undertook a military flying course at Ghedi and graduated as a Sergente Pilota.

He was initially assigned to 366ª *Squadriglia*, 151° *Gruppo*, 53° *Stormo*, but just prior to Italy's entry into World War 2 he was transferred to Trapani, in Sicily, to serve with 384ª *Squadriglia*, 157° *Gruppo*.

Like most of his contemporaries, Martinoli started the war flying the CR.42, and he used the Fiat fighter to claim his first victory – a bomber, which he shot down over Tunis on 13 June 1940. There is some mystery surrounding this kill, for it *(text continues on page 59)*

COLOUR PLATES

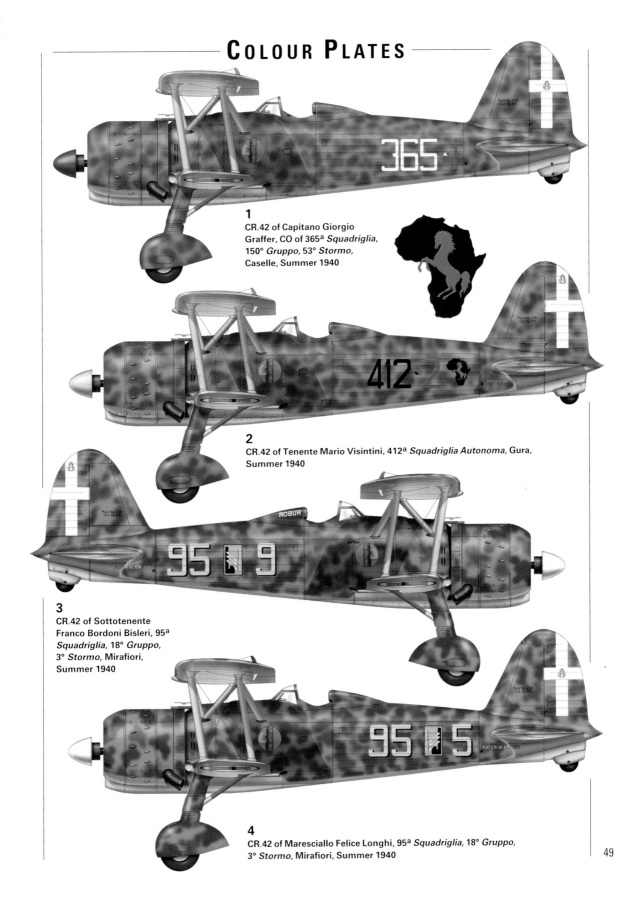

1
CR.42 of Capitano Giorgio
Graffer, CO of 365ª *Squadriglia*,
150° *Gruppo*, 53° *Stormo*,
Caselle, Summer 1940

2
CR.42 of Tenente Mario Visintini, 412ª *Squadriglia Autonoma*, Gura,
Summer 1940

3
CR.42 of Sottotenente
Franco Bordoni Bisleri, 95ª
Squadriglia, 18° *Gruppo*,
3° *Stormo*, Mirafiori,
Summer 1940

4
CR.42 of Maresciallo Felice Longhi, 95ª *Squadriglia*, 18° *Gruppo*,
3° *Stormo*, Mirafiori, Summer 1940

5
C.200 of Sottotenente Franco Bordoni Bisleri, 95ª *Squadriglia*, 18° *Gruppo*,
3° *Stormo*, Atene-Tatoi, October 1941

6
C.200 of Tenente Franco Lucchini, 90ª *Squadriglia*, 10° *Gruppo*, 4° *Stormo*, Catania,
August 1941

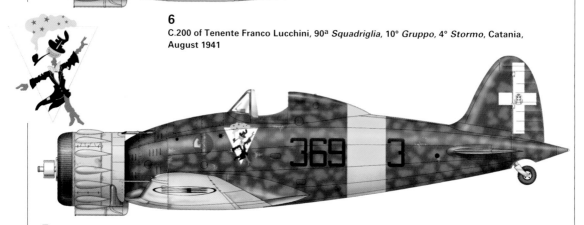

7
C.200 of Sottotenente Giuseppe Biron, 369ª *Squadriglia*, 22° *Gruppo Autonomo*, Krivoj-Rog, September 1941

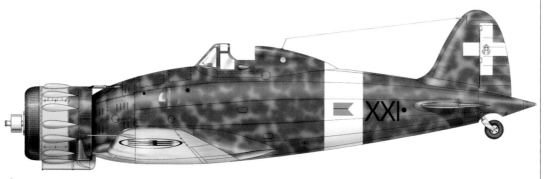

8
C.200 of Maggiore Ettore Foschini, CO of 21° *Gruppo Autonomo*, Stalino, May 1942

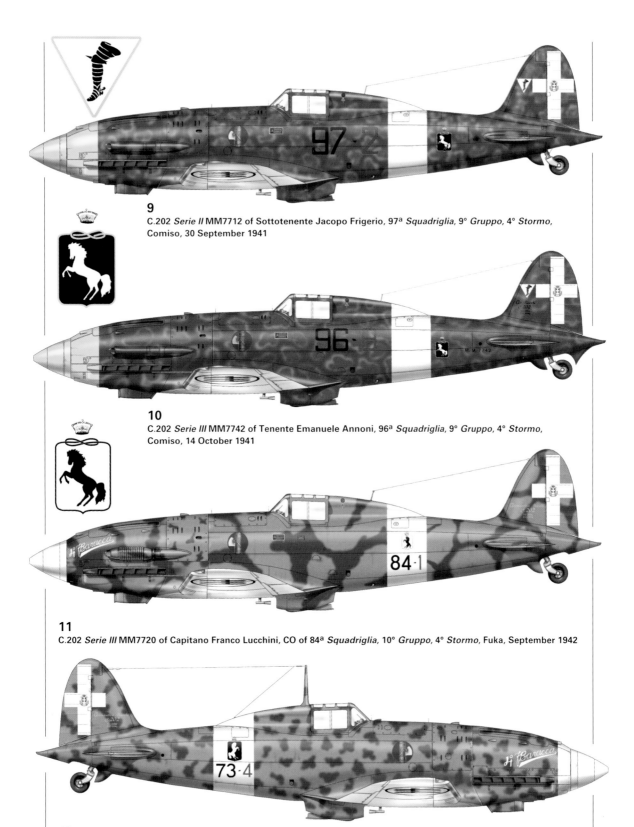

9
C.202 *Serie II* MM7712 of Sottotenente Jacopo Frigerio, 97ª *Squadriglia*, 9° *Gruppo*, 4° *Stormo*, Comiso, 30 September 1941

10
C.202 *Serie III* MM7742 of Tenente Emanuele Annoni, 96ª *Squadriglia*, 9° *Gruppo*, 4° *Stormo*, Comiso, 14 October 1941

11
C.202 *Serie III* MM7720 of Capitano Franco Lucchini, CO of 84ª *Squadriglia*, 10° *Gruppo*, 4° *Stormo*, Fuka, September 1942

12
C.202 *Serie III* MM7764 of Sergente Maggiore Teresio Martinoli, 73ª *Squadriglia*, 9° *Gruppo*, 4° *Stormo*, Gela, July 1942

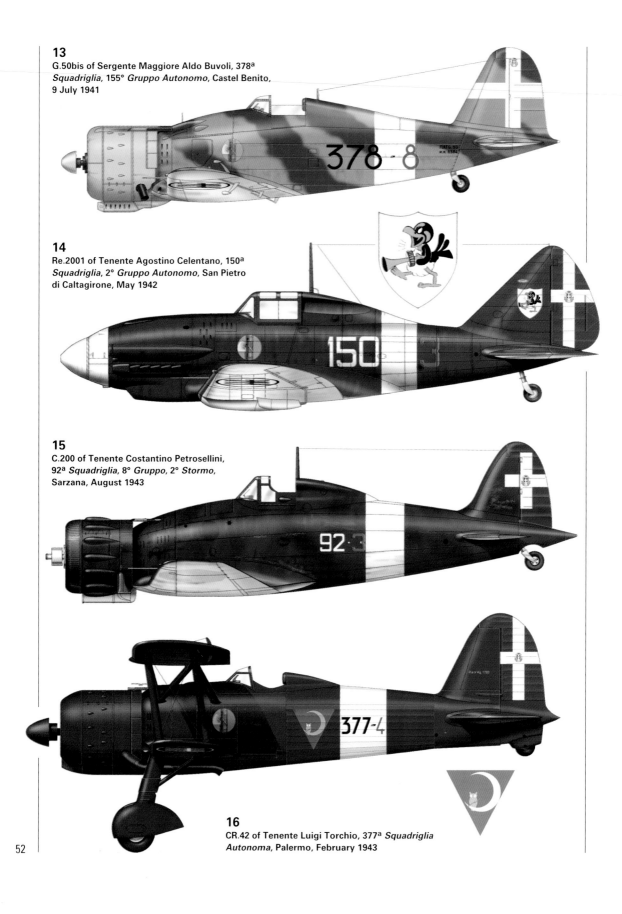

13
G.50bis of Sergente Maggiore Aldo Buvoli, 378ª
Squadriglia, 155° *Gruppo Autonomo*, Castel Benito,
9 July 1941

14
Re.2001 of Tenente Agostino Celentano, 150ª
Squadriglia, 2° *Gruppo Autonomo*, San Pietro
di Caltagirone, May 1942

15
C.200 of Tenente Costantino Petrosellini,
92ª *Squadriglia*, 8° *Gruppo*, 2° *Stormo*,
Sarzana, August 1943

16
CR.42 of Tenente Luigi Torchio, 377ª *Squadriglia*
Autonoma, Palermo, February 1943

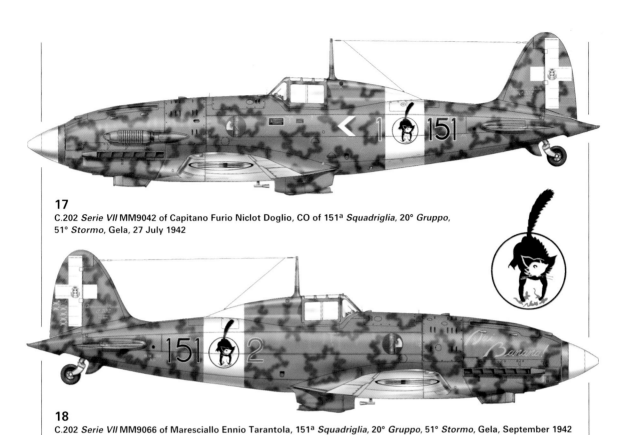

17
C.202 *Serie VII* MM9042 of Capitano Furio Niclot Doglio, CO of 151ª *Squadriglia*, 20° *Gruppo*,
51° *Stormo*, Gela, 27 July 1942

18
C.202 *Serie VII* MM9066 of Maresciallo Ennio Tarantola, 151ª *Squadriglia*, 20° *Gruppo*, 51° *Stormo*, Gela, September 1942

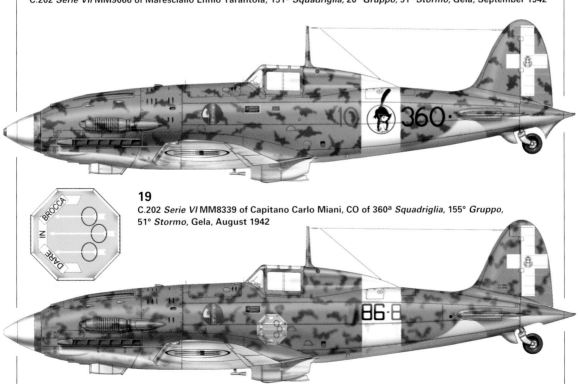

19
C.202 *Serie VI* MM8339 of Capitano Carlo Miani, CO of 360ª *Squadriglia*, 155° *Gruppo*,
51° *Stormo*, Gela, August 1942

20
C.202 *Serie I* MM7944 of Tenente Adriano Visconti, 86ª *Squadriglia*, 7° *Gruppo*, 4° *Stormo*, Pantelleria, May 1942

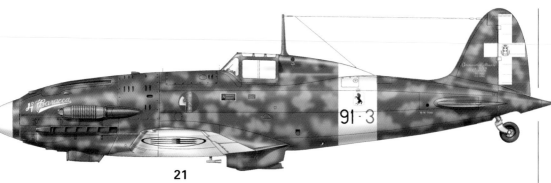

21
C.202 *Serie III* MM7844 of Capitano Carlo Maurizio Ruspoli, CO of 91ª *Squadriglia*,
10° *Gruppo*, 4° *Stormo*, Fuka, September 1942

22
C.202 *Serie III* MM7821 of Tenente Emanuele Annoni, CO of 96ª *Squadriglia*, 9° *Gruppo*,
4° *Stormo*, Fuka, 19 September 1942

23
C.202 *Serie I* MM7910 of Maresciallo Alessandro Bladelli, 91ª *Squadriglia*, 10° *Gruppo*, 4° *Stormo*, Fuka, September 1942

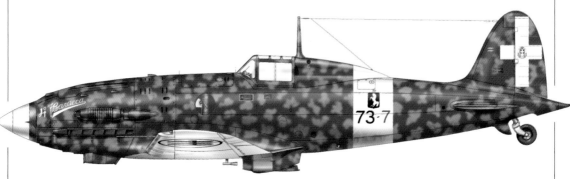

24
C.202 *Serie III* MM7944 of Tenente Giulio Reiner, CO of 73ª *Squadriglia*, 9° *Gruppo*, 4° *Stormo*, Fuka, August 1942

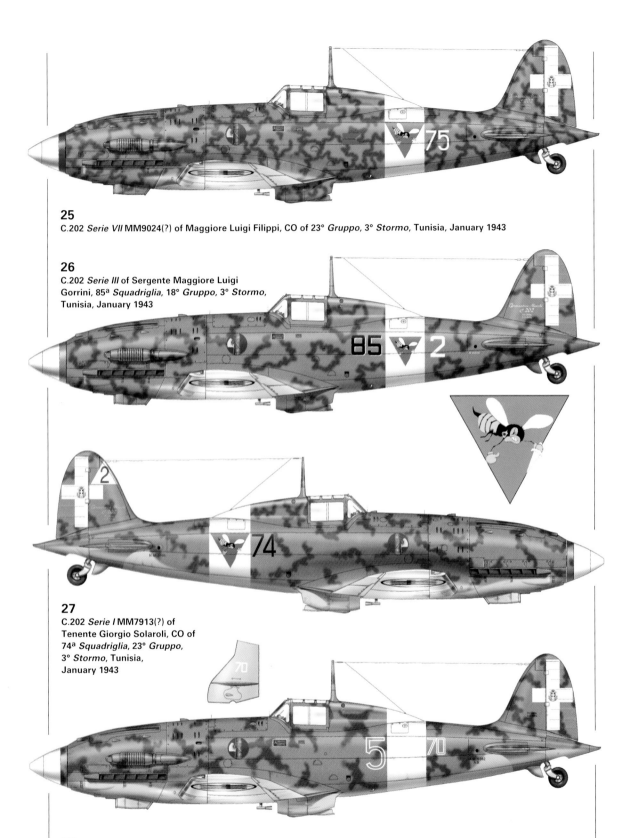

25
C.202 *Serie VII* MM9024(?) of Maggiore Luigi Filippi, CO of 23° *Gruppo*, 3° *Stormo*, Tunisia, January 1943

26
C.202 *Serie III* of Sergente Maggiore Luigi
Gorrini, 85ª *Squadriglia*, 18° *Gruppo*, 3° *Stormo*,
Tunisia, January 1943

27
C.202 *Serie I* MM7913(?) of
Tenente Giorgio Solaroli, CO of
74ª *Squadriglia*, 23° *Gruppo*,
3° *Stormo*, Tunisia,
January 1943

28
C.202 *Serie X* of Capitano Claudio Solaro, CO of 70ª *Squadriglia*, 23° *Gruppo*, 3° *Stormo*, Tunisia, January 1943

29
C.202 *Serie III* of Sottotenente Leonardo Ferrulli, 91ª *Squadriglia*, 10° *Gruppo*, 4° *Stormo*, Fuka, October 1942

30
C.202 *Serie IX* of Sergente Maggiore Walter Omiccioli, 98ª *Squadriglia*, 7° *Gruppo*, 54° *Stormo*, Caselle, April 1943

31
C.202 *Serie X* MM9570 of Capitano Dante Ocarso, CO of 88ª *Squadriglia*, 6° *Gruppo*, 1° *Stormo*, Decimomannu, November 1942

32
C.202 *Serie IX* MM9398 of Maresciallo GianLino Baschirotto, 88ª *Squadriglia*, 6° *Gruppo*, 1° *Stormo*, Pantelleria, December 1942

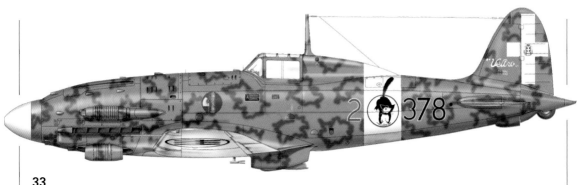

33
C.205V Veltro *Serie III* MM92156 of Sergente Ferruccio Serafini, 378ª *Squadriglia*, 155° *Gruppo Autonomo*, Capoterra,
22 July 1943

34
C.202 *Serie XI* of Tenente Orfeo Mazzitelli, 359ª *Squadriglia*, 22° *Gruppo Autonomo*,
Capodichino, August 1943

35
Bf 109G-6 Wk-Nr 18391 of Capitano Mario Bellagambi, CO of 364ª *Squadriglia*,
150° *Gruppo Autonomo*, Sciacca, June 1943

36
Bf 109G-6 Wk-Nr 18421 of Tenente Ugo Drago, CO of 363ª *Squadriglia*, 150° *Gruppo Autonomo*, Sciacca, June 1943

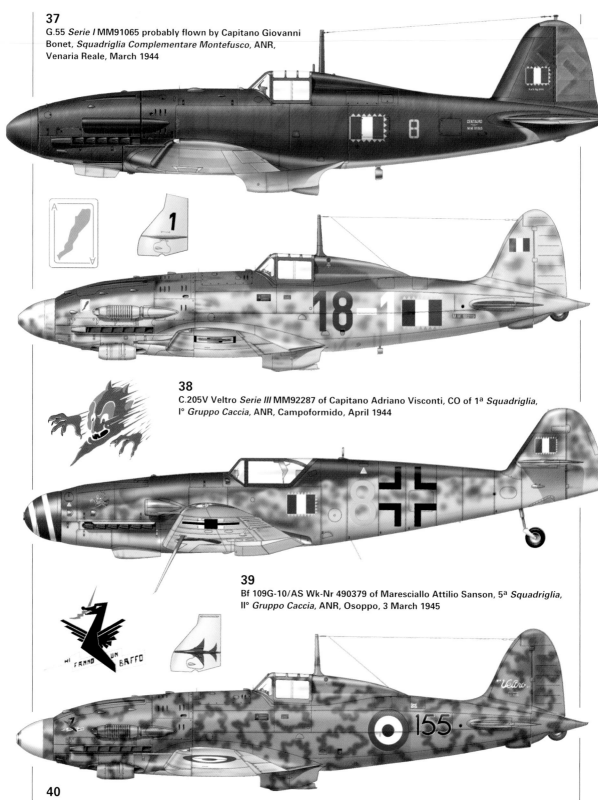

37
G.55 *Serie I* MM91065 probably flown by Capitano Giovanni
Bonet, *Squadriglia Complementare Montefusco*, ANR,
Venaria Reale, March 1944

38
C.205V Veltro *Serie III* MM92287 of Capitano Adriano Visconti, CO of 1ª *Squadriglia*,
I° *Gruppo Caccia*, ANR, Campoformido, April 1944

39
Bf 109G-10/AS Wk-Nr 490379 of Maresciallo Attilio Sanson, 5ª *Squadriglia*,
II° *Gruppo Caccia*, ANR, Osoppo, 3 March 1945

40
C.205V Veltro *Serie III* of Tenente Colonnello Duilio Fanali, CO of 155° *Gruppo, Aeronautica Co-Belligerante*, Lecce,
late 1943

Italian 'ace of aces' during World War 2 was Sergente Maggiore Martinoli, seen here at the extreme right in this group shot of 9° *Gruppo* pilots

C.202 (MM7764) '73-4' was Martinoli's regular mount for much of his second tour of operations in North Africa in 1942. Up on a patrol from Abu Haggag, the ace is seen at the controls of the fighter over typically featureless Egyptian desert in September of that year

cannot be confirmed in any other documentation except for a very precise entry in his own log book. He then joined 78ª *Squadriglia*, 13° *Gruppo*, 2° *Stormo* in Libya, where he again flew CR.42s. Martinoli's second claim took the form of a Gladiator (almost certainly from No 112 Sqn, although RAF records cannot confirm this), which he downed on 13 October whilst escorting a S.79 bomber over Marsa Matruh.

His third, and last, victory in his first African tour was scored after he had transferred to 4° *Stormo* (which then became his permanent unit), Martinoli claiming a Blenheim which went down in the Bardia zone on 5 January 1941.

He failed to achieve any further victories following his unit's return to Italy for re-equipment with the C.200 in early 1941, but dramatically increased his score in the autumn when 9° *Gruppo*, to which he belonged, converted onto C.202s. Flying from the Sicilian base at Comiso on fighter sweeps over Malta, Martinoli claimed three Hurricanes and a Blenheim destroyed in two solid months of action.

9° *Gruppo* then enjoyed a brief winter rest from fighting, before returning to operations over Malta in the spring and early summer of 1942. By then the first Spitfires had arrived on the besieged island, and the C.202 pilots found themselves embroiled in fierce dogfights whilst protecting the Z.1007 and S.84 bombers from Allied fighters. Seeing action on a near daily basis, Martinoli was credited with the individual destruction of three Spitfires (plus a fourth as a probable) between 4 and 16 May.

Towards the end of that same month, the whole *stormo* returned to Africa to participate in Rommel's great offensive. The aces of the 'Fourth' – Lucchini, Ferrulli, Giannella, Veronesi, Malvezzi, Reiner, Annoni and Barcaro, along with Martinoli – claimed the lion's share of their victories during this period of near-constant retreat for the Allies.

Between 29 May and 9 October 1942, Martinoli was credited with destroying eight aircraft in the air (six P-40s and two Spitfires), and on the eve of the British counter-attack (23 October) he downed yet another single-engined aircraft over El Daba – probably a Kittyhawk from No 260 Sqn, although it was officially, and incorrectly, identified as a P-39 Airacobra. This proved to be his final kill in North Africa.

The following year Martinoli was assigned the impossible task of defending his homeland, and during the air battles of the first days of July (which cost the lives of fellow aces Lucchini and Ferrulli), he shared in the destruction of a P-38 and a B-17 whilst flying a C.205V. His last Allied victim was a Spitfire shot down on 15 August, by which time the invading forces had already established a strong foothold in Sicily.

This, however, was not the end of Martinoli's fighting career, for together with most of his colleagues in 4° *Stormo*, he joined the *Aeronautica Co-Belligerante* after the Armistice. This gave him (and a handful of other Italian pilots, including nine-kill ace Emanuele Annoni) the opportunity to shoot down an ex-ally in the form of a Luftwaffe Ju 52/3m over Podgorica, in Yugoslavia, following a dogfight with two escorting Bf 109s.

With 276 combat missions to his credit, Martinoli was finally to lose his life on 25 August 1944 during a training accident whilst converting from the C.205V to the P-39 Airacobra, examples of which had just been delivered to the *Aeronautica Co-Belligerante*.

So ended the life of a pilot who, through the authors' research, is considered to be Italy's top scoring ace of World War 2. Teresio Martinoli, already decorated with two Silver Medals and the German Iron Cross (Second Class), was accorded the Gold Medal for Military Valour following his death.

Fellow ace Giulio Reiner, who was Martinoli's commander during his time with 73ª *Squadriglia*, remembered;

'Behind his discreet and closed character was a fighter pilot who possessed exceptional eyesight, making him an unfailing marksman. In fact, it seemed as if Martinoli had a sixth sense when it came to detecting the enemy's presence, for he would usually spot his position in the sky well before any of us could.'

Franco Lucchini

Born in Rome on Christmas Eve 1914, Lucchini enrolled in the *Regia Aeronautica's* pilot officers' course for 1935 and obtained his 'wings' the following year. In 1937 he volunteered for duty in Spain, where, under the name of Lunigiano, he cut his teeth as a fighter pilot flying with the famous *Asso di Bastoni* (Ace of Clubs) XXIII *Gruppo*. He scored his first personal victory whilst serving with the *Aviazione Legionaria*, and shared in two more.

Lucchini was forced to take to his parachute on two occasions after clashing with enemy fighters over Spain. He successfully evaded capture the first time, but when he repeated the feat on 22 July 1938,

Italy's second ranking ace of World War 2 was Capitano Franco Lucchini, who is seen here posing with his C.202 whilst CO of 84ª *Squadriglia*

Bearing the traditional '1' code worn by the *squadriglia* commander's aircraft, this *Serie III* C.202 (MM7720) was used by Lucchini during 84ª *Squadriglia's* North Africa tour in 1942. The aircraft had already enjoyed an unusually long operational career with the *Regia Aeronautica* by the time it was issued to Lucchini, for it had originally been delivered new to 1° *Stormo* at Campoformido in the autumn of 1941

This rear view shot of C.202 '84-1' reveals that MM7720 had not survived its year in the frontline totally unscathed, however – the aircraft's starboard wing is from a later-production machine, hence the 'smoke-ring' mottled camouflage

On 24 October 1942, Lucchini hastily scrambled from Fuka in this C.202 (MM7919 '84-12') to intercept a large Desert Air Force formation flying in support of the opening phase of the Battle of El Alamein. After sharing in the destruction of a Kittyhawk and a Mitchell with Tenenti Francesco De Seta and Paolo Berti, Lucchini was forced to crash-land his battle-damaged Macchi. He had been badly wounded during this action, and was duly shipped back to Italy to recover

he was taken prisoner by Republican forces and held in Valencia for six months.

Upon returning to Italy, Lucchini was assigned to 4° *Stormo* (which, together with 1° *Stormo*, was traditionally considered to be an elite fighter unit), based at T2 airfield on the outskirts of the Libyan port of Tobruk. Flying CR.42s with 90ª *Squadriglia* of 10° *Gruppo* under the command of Capitano Maggini, his operational debut with the unit, on 14 June 1940, saw the *stormo* claim its first kill. Shared four ways between Maggini, Tenente Guiducci (a close friend of Lucchini from the Spanish Civil War), Sergente Ceoletta and Lucchini, their victim was an RAF Gladiator – no losses are noted in RAF records, however.

Exactly a week later, while conducting a routine escort mission, Lucchini engaged the enemy once again, although this time his quarry was not an equally nimble biplane fighter but a far larger, and well-armed, Sunderland I flying boat from No 230 Sqn. Carrying out an

armed reconnaissance mission to Tobruk, the Sunderland was initially intercepted at dawn by two pilots (Tenenti Piccolomini and Savoia) from 2º *Stormo*, who fired at the flying boat for quite some time. The Sunderland was then attacked by Sergente Steppi of 84ª *Squadriglia* and finally Lucchini, who pressed home his attack and forced the flying boat down in the port of Bardia, where the crew was captured.

The Sunderland was Lucchini's first victory of World War 2, and by the end of his first African tour, he had added two more victories to his tally in the form of a Gladiator and a Hurricane. Early in 1941 4º *Stormo* received C.200s and transferred to Sicily to participate in the Malta raids. During a fiercely fought campaign Lucchini once again showed his talents as both a marksman and determined leader, adding a further four Hurricanes to his tally between June and September .

For Lucchini, this campaign came to an abrupt end when he and several other pilots from his unit were forced to perform a crash-landing on the small island of Ustica due to a navigational error. He suffered serious wounds to his face and one of his arms, and he had to endure a long period of convalescence.

In the autumn of 1941 4º *Stormo* was equipped with the C.202, and a fully recovered Lucchini made full use of the modern Macchi fighter. On 1 December he was given command of 84ª *Squadriglia*, and by early April he was back in Sicily leading his unit in bomber escort missions to Malta – during the new campaign he downed two Spitfires on 5 and 15 May respectively.

4º *Stormo* was sent in its entirety to North Africa in late May, arriving in time to participate in Rommel's summer offensive. Always in the very eye of the action, Lucchini claimed nine aircraft (four Kittyhawks, two Spitfires, two Hurricanes and a Boston) between 4 June and 3 September 1942, and shared in over a dozen other victories. On 20 October he scored another solo victory against a P-40, but four days later he was shot down and badly wounded. Sent home in a critical condition on a hospital ship, Lucchini's war-weary *stormo* followed him back to Italy two months later.

By the spring of 1943, both Lucchini and 4º *Stormo* were once again back in the frontline. In June he took command of 10º *Gruppo*, based in Sicily on various airfields around Catania. Outnumbered every time he led his unit into action, Lucchini claimed his final victory on 5 July when he downed one of the Spitfires providing fighter escort for USAAF B-17s of the 99th Bomb Group (BG) that had been sent to bomb Gerbini. Moments after destroying his foe, Lucchini was caught in the deadly crossfire of the bomber formation, and in full view of his horrified wingman, Tenente Bertolaso, the ace's C.202 fell earthwards out of control. Lucchini's body was found two days later, still entangled in the remains of his aircraft.

Within minutes of Lucchini's death, fellow Spanish Civil War veteran, and 21-kill ace, Sottotenente Leonardo Ferrulli of 4º *Stormo* was also shot down and killed. The *Regia Aeronautica* had lost its second and third ranking aces in a single mission.

Amleto Monterumici, Lucchini's faithful wingman during many a sortie, remembers to this day the strong determination with which the ace took on the enemy, even in the face of great odds;

'He was always ready to fight, and courageously sought out the enemy at every opportunity. As with a great number of fighter pilots, he was blessed with extraordinary eyesight, which meant that he could spot his enemy and anticipate an attack. Although he was serious, withdrawn and occasionally timid when on the ground, in the air he transformed himself into a frightening, and aggressive, fighter.'

In a very rare tribute to his bravery in action, Lucchini's name appears twice in the *Bollettino di Guerra* (despatches), on 5 September 1942 and 6 July 1943. During his career he was decorated with five Silver Medals and one Bronze Medal for Military Valour, three War Crosses and a German Iron Cross (Second Class). As a final posthumous award, he received the Gold Medal for Military Valour for his last aerial combat (his 262nd mission) and his overall achievements as a pilot and unit commander within the *Regia Aeronautica*.

Leonardo Ferrulli

Of the major Italian aces, Leonardo Ferrulli is undoubtedly the least well known. This is partially attributable to his unassuming character, and also to the history of his unit, 91ᵃ *Squadriglia* of 4º *Stormo's* 10º *Gruppo*, which enjoyed great success, but also suffered heavy losses.

Probably the most famous of all the *Regia Aeronautica's* fighter units, the *squadriglia* was named after Italy's ranking ace of World War 1, Maggiore Francesco Baracca. During World War 2 no less than 16 of the unit's pilots were killed in action, and with few 91a *Squadriglia* veterans surviving its numerous campaigns, combat accounts from the unit are hard to find. This lack of information is further compounded by the near-total destruction of the unit's official wartime records.

Therefore, when it came to recounting Ferrulli's career only fragments of information were available, which were cross-checked with accounts from those with personal knowledge of his achievements.

Leonardo Ferrulli was born in Brindisi on 1 January 1918. He enrolled in the air force in 1935 and obtained his wings as a Sergente Pilota in May 1936. His piloting skills were recognised by an assignment to 4º *Stormo*, from where he immediately volunteered for service in Spain. On 7 October 1937 Ferrulli managed to shoot down a Tupolev SB-2 twin-engined bomber (which the Nationalist forces referred to as 'Martin' bomber) after a long chase in his CR.32, the aircraft crashing into the sea off Palma di Majorca. Following the Nationalist victory, and receipt of the Silver Medal for Military Valour, Ferrulli returned to Italy.

He duly became one of the first pilots within the *Regia Aeronautica*

Sottotenente Leonard Ferrulli (seen here as a Sergente Maggiore) was photographed in front of his CR.42 during his first North African tour with 4° *Stormo* in 1940. He claimed six Hurricanes and a Blenheim during this opening phase of the desert war

63

to transition onto the C.200, although his colleagues' predilection for their obsolescent CR.42s meant that 4° *Stormo* entered World War 2 still flying biplane fighters. Ferrulli made full use of his Spanish war experience during his first tour in North Africa, claiming six Hurricanes and a Blenheim destroyed.

Returning to Italy with his *stormo* in January 1941, Ferrulli next saw action over Malta six months later – by which time his unit had fully converted onto the C.200. He scored a solitary kill whilst flying from Sicily, claiming a Hurricane on 4 July 1941. By year-end 4° *Stormo* had received C.202s, and in May 1942 it was sent to North Africa once again to support the new Axis offensive. Over the next five months Ferrulli downed eight P-40s and a Spitfire, and upon returning to Italy in December, he was promoted to Sottotenente.

As previously mentioned, his operational career came to sudden end during the defence of Sicily, when he was shot down by a Spitfire on 5 July 1943. Ferrulli had claimed the destruction of a P-38 just 24 hours earlier, and on the morning of his death, he had scrambled to intercept a formation of 99th BG B-17s. Managing to shoot one of the bombers down, (three Flying Fortresses were lost on this mission) along with an escorting Lightning, he was in turn jumped by a flight of Spitfires that had been patrolling above the B-17s. Ferrulli bailed out of his badly damaged C.202 but it was too low, his parachute failing to deploy before he hit the ground near Scordia. A posthumous Gold Medal for Military Valour was subsequently added to his previous decorations, which included three Silver Medals.

Franco Bordoni Bisleri

Franco Bordoni Bisleri viewed a career in the *Regia Aeronautica* as a way to further his sporting aspirations. Heir to an established family business that was especially famous throughout Italy at that time for its Ferro-China Bisleri liqueur, the young Franco was attracted to flying by the lure of speed.

Born in Milan on 10 January 1913, by the time he had completed his studies at the San Carlo College (one of the most exclusive private schools in the city), Bordoni Bisleri had already shown himself to be a talented racing car driver. Initially prevented from joining the *Regia Aeronautica* due to a minor nasal problem, he continued to pursue a flying career by obtaining a private pilot's licence. He finally succeeded in entering the service in 1937 as a temporary Sottotenente Pilota.

Returning to civilian life once his term of National Service had been served, Bordoni Bisleri rejoined the air force upon Italy's declaration of war. Sent to 18° *Gruppo's* 95ª *Squadriglia*, he participated in the Channel Front campaign in the autumn of 1940 with the *Corpo Aereo Italiano* in Belgium. Here, he soon found that

Perched on the fuselage of his CR.42 (MM5688 '95-9'), Sottotenente Franco Bordoni Bisleri flew this aircraft from Mirafiori in the weeks immediately following the Italian declaration of war. Note that he had his nickname (*ROBUR*) painted on the fighter's headrest

Bordoni Bisleri also had his nickname applied to his C.200 following 18° *Gruppo's* transition to the Macchi fighter in the autumn of 1941. The fighter was photographed at Atene-Tatoi in October 1941

By July 1943 Tenente Bordoni Bisleri was flying a C.205V from Cerveteri, and he enjoyed great success with the Macchi fighter, claiming seven bombers destroyed. Parked behind him is a rare SAI Ambrosini SAI.207 fighter also assigned to 3° *Stormo*

his CR.42 was totally outclassed in all departments, bar manoeuvrability, by the defending RAF Hurricanes and Spitfires.

Upon its return to Italy in January 1941, 18° *Gruppo* was sent to North Africa. The arid desert expanses better suited the Fiat biplane's open cockpit layout, which had offered its pilots no protection whatsoever in the cold and damp conditions regularly encountered in northern Europe.

Bordoni Bisleri, who had his nickname 'Robur' painted onto the headrest of his CR.42 (a name connected with the advertising campaign for his family's famous liqueur!), obtained his first kill on 10 March 1941 when he claimed a Blenheim 100 kilometres east of Benghasi. According to some of the documentation that pertains to this incident, he shared the RAF bomber with Maresciallo Longhi.

Bordoni Bisleri's first African tour ended with two victories in April (a Hurricane on the 14th and a Blenheim on the 17th, the latter being forced down 40 kilometres east of Derna) and two more in June (two Blenheims on the 2nd in the vicinity of Benghasi), after which he was promoted to Tenente. Upon returning to Italy in August, 18° *Gruppo* initially re-equipped with G.50s, although these had been replaced with C.200s by the time it transferred to Greece, where the unit failed to encounter any enemy aircraft.

In July 1942 18° *Gruppo* returned to North Africa as part of 3° *Stormo* to support the latest Axis offensive, with the unit concentrating on flying ground attack missions. Despite this change of roles, Bordoni Bisleri still managed to display his skill as a fighter pilot by shooting down six P-40s and a Boston between 20 October and 7 November. Ironically, having survived countless combat missions, he was injured in car accident on 19 November and sent home on a hospital ship.

Following a long period of convalescence, Bordoni Bisleri returned to active service with 3° *Stormo* at Cerveteri in June 1943. Flying the faster, and better armed, C.205V Veltro, the unit was tasked with defending central Italy, and Rome in particular. Bordoni Bisleri duly added six B-17s and a B-26 to his tally during incessant interceptions between 30 July and 5 September, and together with his colleague 'Gigi' Gorrini, he undoubtedly became the hero of the *Regia Aeronautica's* final campaign.

The Armistice of 8 September brought his career to an end, and together with Gorrini, he is the top scoring Italian ace (19 victories) to have survived the war. Bordoni Bisleri's decorations include three Silver Medals for Military Valour and an Iron Cross, Second Class. After the war he returned to his family business and dedicated his life to sportscar racing, winning several titles including the Italian Championship in the sportscar category in 1953.

Bordoni Bisleri lost his life in a light aeroplane crash on 15 September 1975 when his single-engined SIAI Marchetti F.260 crashed into Mount Anchetta, near Chiavari in Liguria, during bad weather. With him was his ten-year-old son Francesco and friend Gianni Allegri. The ace was returning to Milan from Rome following an audience with His Holiness Pope Paul VI on the occasion of a parachutists' commemoration organised by the Milan Aero Club, of which he was President. Franco Bordoni Bisleri's tragic demise created considerable press coverage at the time, although little was mentioned of his glorious past with the *Regia Aeronautica*.

Giorgio Solaroli di Briona

Giorgio Solaroli Marchese of Briona joined the *Regia Aeronautica* because of the rich military tradition within his family. Beginning with his great-grandfather Paolo, who had fought throughout the Risorgimento War, members of his family had been awarded all manner of Italian military decorations, including nine Medals for Military Valour (three Gold and six Bronze).

Born in Turin on 17 July 1918, Solaroli applied to join the *Accademia Aeronautica* at Caserta as soon as he had finished college, and was enrolled in the *'Sparviero'* course. Graduating in July 1940, he was given the rank of Sottotenente Pilota and sent to Castiglione del Lago for fighter training. He then joined 95ª *Squadriglia*, 18º *Gruppo*, 3º *Stormo*, which subsequently moved to Belgium to participate in the CAI expedition.

On returning home, Solaroli moved to 3º *Stormo's* 23º *Gruppo*, and saw action over Malta with the unit in March 1941. Here, he enjoyed his first taste of command at the head of 377ª *Squadriglia Autonoma*, which had been given the task of combat-testing the new Re.2000 fighter. Although the Reggiane design failed to live up to the high expectations which had surrounded its development, it

Tenente Giorgio Solaroli di Briona poses alongside an Re.2000 of 377ª *Squadriglia Autonoma* in Sicily in the autumn of 1941. The future ace completed three hazardous fighter-bomber missions at night over Malta with the Reggiane in November and December of that year

Aircraft and personnel of 3° *Stormo* are seen between sorties at Abu Haggag in the autumn of 1942. The C.202 nearest to the camera ('74-2') was often flown by Solaroli during this period of intense action in North Africa. Contrary to standard practice, the aircraft's individual number code '2' has been painted onto the fin within a white triangle, rather than applied aft of the fuselage band

Only Tenente Solaroli seems willing to smile for the camera at El Hamma, in Tunisia, following his receipt of the Iron Cross, second class, on 11 February 1943. Admittedly, neither he or his fellow 3° *Stormo* pilots Tenente Specker and Capitano Claudio Solaro (10 kills) had a lot to be happy about, as they fought in vain to protect the retreating axis forces from the Desert Air Force

nevertheless offered Solaroli the chance to test the aircraft in the fighter-bomber role. He duly flew three highly dangerous missions over Malta on the nights of 15 and 19 November and 1 December 1941.

In his diary, Solaroli wrote down a vivid account of his experiences, highlighting one specific deficiency in the training of all Italian fighter pilots – an absolute lack of blind/instrument-flight instruction.

He returned to 74ª *Squadriglia* in 1942, moving to Abu Haggag, in Libya, with the unit (now flying C.202s) in July in order to take part in the summer offensive. On 4 September, whilst on a routine patrol over the frontline at about 4000 metres, his flight (under the command of Capitano Giorgio Tugnoli, who was to end the war with five victories) encountered a formation of Bostons, heavily escorted by P-40s. Solaroli's diary recorded the action which ensued;

'My wingman, Sergente Maggiore Mantelli, and I swept down onto the left flank of the escort. I immediately began to fire at a P-40 which filled my gunsight. There was absolutely no reaction from the English pilot – so much so that I got to within a few metres before I saw him explode, turn on his back and crash into the ground. I vigorously pulled up, for I had to avoid other enemy fighters which were snapping at my heels. With the speed I had gained in the dive I soon found myself at a favourable altitude to attack another formation. This time I again managed to machine-gun a P-40 at close quarters. I hit the aircraft and observed that it caught fire.'

But the fight was far from over, for Solaroli's fighter had been hit by numerous rounds fired by Sgt N D Stebbings in his No 260 Sqn Kittyhawk. Despite his C.202 being set on fire, and with wounds to his head and one of his legs, Solaroli chose not to abandon the aircraft, instead managing to regain friendly territory before crash-landing. Extricating himself from his fighter, the ace limped off westwards in search of help;

'Finally, I saw three men waving their hands at me, telling me not to move as they carefully made their way towards me. They explained that I had landed in a minefield – it must have been pure luck that I had not blown the whole place up!'

Four C.202s from 23° *Gruppo* prepare for take-off from El Hamma in early February 1943. The aircraft in the foreground ('70-5') was regularly flown by the CO of 70ª *Squadriglia*, Capitano Claudio Solaro, during this period. One of the most experienced pilots in the *Regia Aeronautica*, Solaro commanded this unit from July 1940 through to the end of 1943. A Spanish war veteran (where he scored a single kill over an I-16), his most successful period in terms of aerial victories came during the final months of combat in Tunisia, when he was credited with eight victories

Solaroli rejoined his unit following a month in a camp hospital in Libya, and he celebrated his return on 20 October by sharing in the destruction of two P-40s with Sergente Mandolesi and Capitano Pinna. One of the Allied pilots reported missing on this day was Sgt Stebbings of No 260 Sqn.

Promoted to Capitano in the autumn, Solaroli assumed command of 18° *Gruppo's* 95ª *Squadriglia* on 3 December. Fighting a continual rearguard action throughout the early months of 1943, and shifting bases five times in just seven weeks, Solaroli nevertheless managed to claim two Spitfires, a P-38 and a B-26 between 8 January and 23 March. Virtually bereft of aircraft, the *stormo* then returned home to re-equip in anticipation of the invasion of Italy.

Solaroli's unit was one of those given the direct responsibility of defending Rome, and in the final weeks of fighting he added four P-38s to his tally – the last of these was credited to him on 3 September, just five days prior to the Armistice.

After the war Solaroli dedicated himself to running his family's agricultural business, and for many years he also presided over the Turin Aero Club. The great ace finally passed away in 1996, having added two Silver Medals and one Bronze Medal for Military Valour, as well as an Iron Cross, Second Class, to his family's already impressive collection of decorations.

Fernando Malvezzi

Born at Noceto, in the province of Parma, on 22 October 1912, Fernando Malvezzi displayed a strong, impulsive and exuberant character from an early age. Favouring sports to school work, he abandoned his medical studies at university in response to a call for applications for officer pilots within the *Regia Aeronautica*. Gaining his 'wings' in December 1935, Malvezzi initially served with 3° *Stormo's* 85ª *Squadriglia*. Moving to 116ª *Squadriglia*, where he flew reconnaissance aircraft, he participated in the Ethiopian campaign.

This brief taste of combat flying fuelled Malvezzi's passion for air force life, and upon returning to Italy he decided to undertake a course at the school of air warfare in Florence to secure a permanent commission. On the completion of this course he was assigned to the flying school at Foligno as an instructor, before returning to 85ª *Squadriglia*.

Just prior to the outbreak of war Malvezzi was chosen to become a dive-bomber pilot, or *Picchiatello* as they were nicknamed in Italy. His training involved being sent to the Luftwaffe dive-bombing school at Graz, where he learnt to fly the Junkers Ju 87 Stuka. Following a short, intense course, he was one of the first pilots cleared to fly the Ju 87B-2s and R-2s that had been issued to 96° *Gruppo Autonomo Bombardamento a Tuffo* (Autonomous Dive Bomber Group).

Given temporary command of 236ª *Squadriglia*, Tenente Malvezzi first saw action in September 1940 when the Italian Stukas attacked naval and ground targets in, and around, Malta (see *Osprey Combat Aircraft 6 - Ju 87 Stukageschwader in the Mediterranean and North Africa* for further details). He then led the *squadriglia* in action on the Greek front between October 1940 and early January 1941, before moving to Castelbenito. Flying numerous sorties against Royal Navy vessels off the North African coast, Malvezzi succeeded in hitting the cruiser HMS *Southampton* with 500-lb bombs, on 10 January 1941. The mission was cited in despatches the following day;

'A section of three *picchiatelli*, with Tenente Malvezzi in command, together with Sergente Maggiore Mazzei and Sergente Crespi, hit the cruiser with high calibre bombs.'

Another important cycle of operations followed against the port of Tobruk, and on 11 April Malvezzi's Stuka was hit by anti-aircraft fire during a formation attack. He force-landed short of his airfield due to the damage sustained by the Stuka's engine, although the pilot only suffered light injuries. Two days later he performed his last dive-bombing sortie, his flight log reading 'Dive-bombing attack against ships steaming across Tobruk. One vessel hit'.

Upon returning home on leave, Malvezzi obtained permission to return to the fighter community, and on 28 July 1941 he transferred to 96ª *Squadriglia*, 9° *Gruppo*, 4° *Stormo*, which was converting onto the C.202 at the time. The former Stuka pilot was enthusiastic about his new mount, recalling 'it was master of the sky up to 7000 metres – above that, the Spitfire had the edge'.

On 22 November Malvezzi scored his first kills when he claimed a pair of Hurricanes over Malta. The following day, the unit moved to Libya for a short, but intense, cycle of operations. On his very first day of combat (26 November) as a fighter pilot in this theatre, Malvezzi was credited with a P-40, followed by another over Bir el Gobi on 1 December. Three weeks later the unit returned to Italy to replenish its fighter stocks.

In April 9° *Gruppo* transferred to Sicily to participate in yet another Axis campaign against Malta, although it returned to Tripoli the following month. The unit moved as far east as Fuka, in Egypt, in late June 1942.

Promoted to Capitano at this time, Malvezzi assumed command of 97ª *Squadriglia*, and between 8

9° **Gruppo** was fortunate to have commanding officers of the quality of Tenente Emanuele Annoni (left) and Tenente Fernando Malvezzi leading its *squadrilie* during the critical phase of the North African campaign between June and November 1942. Both aces exhibited great extremes of temperament, Malvezzi being impulsive, exhuberant and extremely self-confident, while 'Ele' Annoni, who was nicknamed 'il Cardinale' ('the Cardinale'), had a calm, authoritative and poised personality. Annoni claimed nine kills during the conflict and Malvezzi ten

June and 20 October, he downed four P-40s, a Maryland and a Spitfire, increasing his tally of individual kills to ten.

During the last of these successful engagements, his engine was hit, forcing him to perform an emergency landing on the beach at El Alamein. Suffering serious facial injuries during the crash-landing, Malvezzi was sent back to Italy to recuperate, although he returned to his unit in early December. A month later 4° *Stormo* abandoned African territory for good, and the ace next saw action over Sicily in June 1943. Evacuating back to Italy once again in mid-July, Malvezzi contracted malaria, forcing him to leave his *stormo*.

Having joined the ANR following the Armistice, he was given command of III° *Gruppo Caccia*, but the unit never saw action – its training on the Bf 109 was completed just as the war came to an end. In post-war years Malvezzi established a successful trucking business which he continues to runs to this day, although he still finds time to fly his SIAI Marchetti 260 with the Parma Aero Club.

Fernando Malvezzi was decorated with three Silver Medals for Military Valour, one Bronze and an Iron Cross, Second Class.

Giulio Reiner

Giuilio Reiner was born in Como on 12 April 1915. A conscientious student and an enthusiastic athlete, by the time he obtained his diploma in 1935 he was already in possession of a private pilot's licence from the Como Aero Club. He then volunteered to join the *Regia Aeronautica* as a temporary officer, and on completing his training was assigned to 199ª *Squadriglia Bombardamento Marittimo* (Maritime Bomber Squadron), flying S.55 flying boats.

Giving up his rank of Sottotenente in order to attend the *'Rex'* course at the *Accademia Aeronautica*, Reiner performed brilliantly (classified 9th out of 303 students), and in July 1939 he once more acquired the grade of Sottotenente, although this time as a permanent officer. He then joined CR.42-equipped 73ˢ *Squadriglia*, 9° *Gruppo*, 4° *Stormo*, and at the end of June 1940 he moved with the unit to Sicily to participate in the opening raids on Malta. The following month the *stormo* moved to North Africa, where Reiner scored his first two kills.

The first of these successes was claimed during a routine armed reconnaissance patrol along the Allied frontline on the evening of 12 October 1940, Reiner accompanying his *gruppo* commander, the famous Maggiore Ernesto Botto. The latter had returned to active duty in spite of having lost his right leg as a result of a wound inflicted in combat over Spain exactly three years earlier. Botto had subsequently earned a Gold Medal for Military Valour, as well as the unique nickname 'Gamba di Ferro' ('Iron Leg').

Tenente Giulio Reiner, commander of 73ª *Squadriglia* (9° *Gruppo*, 4° *Stormo*), poses for a 'moody' shot alongside his C.202 at Castelbenito in early January 1943

Having completed an uneventful patrol, the two pilots were approaching their El Adem base when they spotted three Blenheims preparing to bomb the airfield. They immediately attacked. Following a long and drawn-out encounter, Reiner was credited with two bombers destroyed and Botto one. RAF records fail to confirm these claims, however, stating that three No 55 Sqn Blenheims returned to base with 'battle damage'.

The *stormo* was sent back to Italy on Christmas Day 1940 in order to commence its re-equipment with C.200s. Prior to Reiner seeing further combat with the Macchi, he was transferred to the *Centro Sperimentale* (Experimental Test Centre) at Guidonia, where new prototypes were tested. Remaining there for over a year, he was heavily involved in the shipboard catapult-launch trials of the Re.2000.

In July 1942 Reiner returned to take command of 73ª *Squadriglia*, which had been supporting the renewed Axis campaign in North Africa since late May. During the course of his second tour he shot down seven aircraft (four Spitfires, a P-40, a Boston and a Wellington) in the space of six months. Fleeing from Tripoli in January 1943, 73ª *Squadriglia* next saw action over Sicily in June. Promoted to the rank of Capitano, Reiner claimed a P-38 on 13 July, which took his tally to ten individual kills, eight probables and three destroyed on the ground.

Following the Armistice, he shared in the fortunes of 4º *Stormo* within the *Aeronautica Co-Belligerante*, seeing action in the Balkans. Eventually attaining the rank of Maggiore due to his wartime service, Reiner ended the conflict with a Silver Medal for Military Valour and an Iron Cross, Second Class, with two citations for further Silver Medals being lost in the chaos following the Armistice – this was not untypical during those final months of war.

Giulio Reiner, who left the service in 1949, continues to work as an engineer in Como to this day, regularly flying at the local aero club.

Carlo Maurizio Ruspoli di Poggio Suasa

Carlo Ruspoli, Prince of Poggio Suasa, and heir to an ancient title of nobility through his Roman family, can be best described as a true 'officer and a gentleman'.

Born at Oberhofen on 25 August 1906, Ruspoli was enrolled into the cavalry regiment as per a long-standing family tradition. However, in 1936 he obtained his pilot's licence at Cameri and applied for a transfer to the air force, taking advantage of a request by the *Regia Aeronautica* for recruits from other branches of the armed services.

Ruspoli was posted to 81ª *Squadriglia*, 6º *Gruppo*, 1º *Stormo*, based in Sicily, soon after Italy entered the war, and he scored his first kill over the Mediterranean on 27 October 1940. A unique aspect of this victory was that the pilot captured the event on ciné film, Ruspoli having installed a camera in the wing leading edge of his C.200.

Although he had initially fitted the camera so as to document 'his war' on a strictly amateur basis, the prince was soon given an official sanction to carry out this undertaking. Indeed, a special *Sezione Volo Fotocinematografica* (Aerial Cinematographic Section) was established within the *Regia Aeronautica*, and Ruspoli was placed in command of

it! He duly filmed operations both in Greece and Russia, and during the latter campaign his modified C.200 was 'jumped' by a pair of I 16s on 27 August 1941. In the ensuing dogfight Ruspoli succeeded in shooting both of his assailants down, although he later had to perform an emergency landing due to the damage inflicted on his own aircraft.

In June 1942 Capitano Ruspoli was transferred to 4° *Stormo* in North Africa, assuming command of the famous 91ª *Squadriglia Baracca* upon his arrival. He subsequently participated in numerous aerial engagements with the Desert Air Force, culminating in the Battle of El Alamein. Between 17 July, when he claimed a Hurricane, and 20 October, when he destroyed three P-40s in two separate dogfights, he added seven kills to his tally.

Although Ruspoli was fortunate enough to survive the bloody battle of El Alamein, his two brothers, Tenente Colonnello Marescotti and Capitano Costantino, were not. Both were parachutists with the *Folgore* regiment, and they were each posthumously decorated with the Gold Medal for Military Valour.

On being promoted to Maggiore, the prince returned to Rome to serve in the *Stato Maggiore* (Air Ministry). During the immediate post-Armistice period, he did his utmost to avoid the total breakdown of air force units. Boasting a degree in law, and fluent in three languages, Ruspoli was drafted in as interpreter at the talks held between Gen Badoglio and Gen Dwight Eisenhower on board HMS *Nelson* on 29 September.

It was during this meeting that the Italian authorities decided to perform a gesture which would capture public opinion. This took the form of a leaflet-dropping raid over Nazi-occupied Rome, which the government hoped would prove to all Italians that they had not abandoned them. Ruspoli,

Flown by Capitano Carlo Ruspoli during his time as CO of 73ª *Squadriglia*, C.202 '91-3' MM7848 was specially modified to carry a cine-camera in the leading edge of its starboard wing. The ace used this aircraft to down most of the seven kills he claimed between July and October 1942 in North Africa

Promoted to Maggiore, and now siding with the Allies, Ruspoli participated in a leaflet-dropping flight over Rome (accompanied by five-kill ace Maggiore Luigi Mariotti) on 6 October 1943. He is seen here packing his 'ordnance' into the cavity between the flaps and the upper wing surface of his C.205V (MM92214). Once over German-occupied Rome, Ruspoli selected flaps down and the leaflets dropped away. Note the fighters's roundel, reinstated by the *Regia Aeronautica* on 21 September 1943

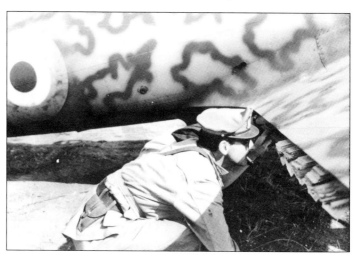

then liaison officer at Allied Command, together with Mariotti and Piccolomini (commanders of the 9º and 10º *Gruppi* respectively, and both fighter aces) were chosen for this unusual mission.

Gaps between the flaps of their C.205Vs were duly packed with leaflets at Brindisi on 6 October 1943, the pilots releasing their 'cargo' simply by lowering the moveable flying surfaces when over Rome. Piccolomini was forced to land at Foggia en route due to technical problems with his aircraft, but Ruspoli and Mariotti successfully completed their mission.

Almost certainly the oldest Italian fighter pilot to become an ace, Ruspoli was decorated with three Silver Medals for Military Valour and an Iron Cross, Second Class. He died in 1947.

GianLino Baschirotto

Maresciallo Baschirotto is the only Italian fighter pilot to have attained ace status twice, achieving this unique feat both in the Spanish Civil War and World War 2.

Born in Montagnana, in the province of Padova, on 15 August 1914, he was fascinated by flying from an early age. He had obtained a civil pilot's licence prior to enrolling in the *Regia Aeronautica*, and upon graduating as a Sergente in 1935, Baschirotto was assigned to 1º *Stormo Caccia*. In August of the following year he became one of the original members of the *Aviacion Legionaria*, volunteering for service in Spain, and flying with the *'Cucaracha'* unit. During ten months of near-solid combat, Baschirotto downed five Republican aircraft.

On his return to Italy, he was one of the most mature, and decorated, pilots in his unit, having been awarded two Silver Medals and a Bronze Medal for Military Valour.

Baschirotto was serving with 88ª *Squadriglia*, 6º *Gruppo*, 1º *Stormo* when Italy declared war, his unit being one of the few to have transitioned onto the C.200. Based at Catania, in Sicily, the *stormo* was immediately involved in the action during bomber escort missions to Malta. Despite completing an intensive cycle of missions over the beleaguered island, followed by months of flying in North Africa,

Dressed for the summer weather, Sergente Maggiore GianLino Baschirotto stands alongside his C.200 (MM5797 '88-9') on Catania in August 1940. The ace's Macchi fighter is an early *Serie II* machine, fitted with an enclosed rear-sliding hood

Baschirotto failed to score his first individual victory until 25 May 1942, by which time he was flying a C.202. With his 'duck' broken, the Spanish War ace went on to claim a further four kills (two P-40s and two Hurricanes) by 10 June.

Having enjoyed great success with the new Macchi fighter over Libya and Egypt between June 1941 and June 1942, 1º *Stormo* was transferred to Pantelleria from Italy to take part in the Tunisian campaign in January 1943. Baschirotto claimed a Beaufighter within days of arriving back in North Africa whilst flying a convoy protection patrols for Axis troop ships traversing the Mediterranean. His sixth, and last, individual victory was against a Spitfire, which he shot down whilst flying a C.205V near Pantelleria on 20 April 1943.

When the Armistice was announced, Baschirotto's *stormo* was re-equipping at Campoformido, near Udine, and he did not participate in any further wartime operations. Apart from the decorations for his service in Spain, he received a further two Silver Medals for Military Valour and an Iron Cross, Second Class, together with a commission for meritorious service.

Many years after the war Baschirotto became a founder member of the *Aeronautica Militare's* first aerobatic display team, and he flew all manner of fast jets then in Italian service. He finally left the air force in 1970 as a Colonnello, and eventually passed away in Vicenza in 1986.

MALTA AND THE MEDITERRANEAN

Furio Niclot Doglio

Born in Cagliari on 24 April 1908, Furio Niclot Doglio had already become a practising aeronautical engineer by the time he obtained his civil pilot's licence in 1930. Thanks to his qualifications, he was immediately employed by the *Compania Nazionale Aeronautica*, based at Rome's Littorio airport, as a test pilot and instructor at the local flying school. He acquired his first world record (altitude record for touring-class floatplanes) on 28 December 1932, and this was followed by other records flights in 1933, during which time he also completed his term of national service with the *Regia Aeronautica* as a non-commissioned Sottotenente Pilota.

Upon his release from duty Niclot moved to Breda, in Milan, as chief test pilot, and in 1935 he carried away the top prize during the Littorio rally in a Breda Ba.33. In 1937 he broke the world speed record over 100 and 1000 kilometres flying the prototype Breda Ba.88. Niclot also received a Silver Medal for Aeronautical Valour for successfully landing a Breda Ba.64 that had suffered mechanical failure.

With Italy's declaration of war, Furio Niclot Doglio (who had meanwhile been promoted to Capitano as a result of his extraordinary achievements) requested a return to active service. He was duly assigned to 353ª *Squadriglia*, 20º *Gruppo*, 51º *Stormo*, which participated in the CAI expedition to Belgium. 20º *Gruppo*, equipped with the G.50, never had any real opportunity to engage the enemy on the Channel Front, and returned to Italy in early 1941.

The unit was subsequently transferred to North Africa in April, and on 30 June Niclot scored his

Capitano Furio Niclot Doglio, CO of 151ª *Squadriglia*, with his his C.202 at Gela in July 1942. His aircraft features a small chevron on either side of the fuselage, denoting in this instance that it was flown by the unit commander. Niclot scored his last two kills over Malta in this machine on 2 and 13 July 1942 – he claimed six Spitfire victories in total during this period

An overall view of Capitano Doglio's C.202 MM9043 '151-1', which he flew in action over Malta whilst commanding 151ª *Squadriglia* (20° *Gruppo*, 51° *Stormo*) in 1942

first victory when he claimed a Hurricane in the vicinity of Ras Azzas while escorting a flight of German Ju 87s.

On 20 November he was appointed commander of 151ª *Squadriglia*, and returned home with his unit exactly a month following the Battle of Marmarica. The *squadriglia* converted onto the C.202 upon its return to Italy, and then deployed to Sicily. Flying from Gela, Niclot's 'war' against Malta was to last just a month, during which time he claimed six individual Spitfire victories between 2 and 13 July 1942, and shared a further two fighters with his faithful wingman, Maresciallo Tarantola. These kills made Niclot Italy's most successful fighter pilot of the 1942 campaign.

On 27 July Niclot fought his last battle in the skies over Malta. Misunderstanding a signal by his wingman, and intent on intercepting another section of RAF fighters immediately ahead of him, he failed to notice a group of Spitfires approaching from his left. A burst fire from the Spitfire V flown by Flt Sgt George 'Buzz' Beurling found its target, Canada's 'ace of aces' later stating in his combat report, 'the poor devil simply blew to pieces in the air'. Cannon rounds had hit the Macchi's engine, and the aircraft immediately caught fire, trapping the pilot inside. Capitano Niclot fell to his death in the sea below and his body was never found. He was Beurling's 14th victory (out of 31 and 1 shared in total), and the second of four victims (two C.202s and two Bf 109s) claimed on this mission.

Furio Niclot Doglio was posthumously awarded the Gold Medal for Military Valour and promoted to the rank of Maggiore for his meritorious service record. In previous campaigns he had already received a Silver Medal and two Bronze Medals, together with the Iron Cross, Second Class.

Ennio Tarantola

Born in Como on 19 January 1915, Ennio Tarantola was universally known throughout the air force as 'Banana' due to his previous employment selling the fruit in Piazza Cavour in his home town! He soon grew tired of this, and joined the *Regia Aeronautica* as a Sergente Pilota in September 1936. Seeing action in the Spanish Civil War as a volunteer within *XVI Gruppo 'Cucaracha'*, Tarantola shot down an

I-15 on 20 January 1938. Upon his return to Italy he joined the CR.32-equipped 155ª *Squadriglia*, and was still serving with the unit when war was declared.

Tarantola's first operational sorties were not to be flown in fighters, however, for he was transferred to a Ju 87 unit within days of Italy going to war. One of a handful of fighter pilots chosen for the elite dive-bomber force due to his acknowledged flying abilities, he spent eight months with 102º *Gruppo 'Bombardamento a Tuffo'* (209ª and 239ª *Squadriglie*) under the command of veteran Spanish war ace, Capitano Giuseppe Cenni.

On 24 June 1941 Tarantola scored a direct hit on the destroyer HMAS *Waterhen*, which was attacked off the North African coast – the vessel subsequently sank after follow-up German raids. The very next day, his Stuka was shot down and he spent 18 hours bobbing around in his liferaft before being rescued. Following this experience he decided to return to fighters, and on 4 November 1941 he joined the G.50-equipped 151ª *Squadriglia*, under the command of Capitano Furio Niclot Doglio. Based in Tripoli, Maresciallo Tarantola claimed his first victory of World War 2 on 5 December 1941 when he downed a P-40.

Early in 1942 151ª *Squadriglia*, as part of 20º *Gruppo*, was transferred to the newly-reformed 51º *Stormo* at Ciampino. Following transition onto the C.202, the unit moved to Gela, in Sicily, in June, and immediately commenced operations against Malta. Tarantola soon forged a strong combat relationship with his commanding officer Niclot, flying as his wingman until the latter's death on 27 July (see previous ace biography). In the month prior to this they had claimed 11 Spitfires destroyed, six falling to Niclot and three to Tarantola, with the remaining two being shared.

Despite being deeply shocked by the loss of his CO, Tarantola continued to fight doggedly over Malta, and in October he added a further two Spitfires to his tally. During another duel that month (on the 14th) his aircraft was so badly shot up that he contemplated taking to his parachute. However, remembering his previous experience in the 'drink' during his Ju 87 days, he remained in the stricken fighter long enough to reach Sicily.

20º *Gruppo* was pulled back to Ciampino Sud in December, and following five months of rest and re-equipment, it was thrown back into the action from Capoterra, in Sardinia, in May 1943. On 20 June Tarantola claimed a P-40 and on 30 July a P-38. Three days later he was involved in the epic battle over Capo Pula, his log book recording that he flew no less than five operational sorties on 2 August. After bouncing a formation of P-40s from the 325th FG, he then engaged P-38s from the

Before becoming a fighter pilot, Maresciallo Tarantola saw action flying Ju 87 dive-bombers with 209ª *Squadriglia* (102º Gruppo) against Allied shipping in the Mediterranean. With fingers gripping the hand hold and one foot firmly planted on the step up, Tarantola prepares to climb up into the cockpit of his Stuka

Now flying fighters, Tarantola stands with fellow 20° *Gruppo* ace, and Gold Medal for Military Valour recipient, Maresciallo Pietro Bianchi in front of the former's C.202 (bearing the inscription *Dai Banana!* on the nose)

A close-up portrait of Maresciallo Pietro Bianchi (five individual victories) sat in the open cockpit of his G.50. The 352ª *Squadriglia* (20° *Gruppo*) pilot was posthumously awarded the Gold Medal for Military Valour following his death in action over Sardinia on 2 August 1943

14th FG, claiming two of them shot down. He lost his friend, and fellow ace, Maresciallo Pietro Bianchi during one of these actions, the fallen pilot later being posthumously decorated with the Gold Medal for Military Valour.

Following the Armistice Tarantola joined the *Squadriglia Complementare 'Montefusco-Bonet'* within the ANR. He had another brush with his old rivals from the 325th FG on 25 April 1944, the American group now flying P-47D Thunderbolts. He found himself on the receiving end this time, however, being forced to bail out of his ailing G.55 fighter. Badly injured in the process, Tarantola did not return to flying until well after VE-Day.

Remaining in the air force until he reached retirement age, Tarantola today remembers that 'once the wheels left the ground, one's rank did not matter any longer – the only thing that mattered was who was the best fighter pilot'. Decorated with four Silver Medals and Two Bronze for Military Valour, he currently resides in Cesenatico, where all those who know him still call him 'Banana'.

Walter Omiccioli

Born in Fano on 12 March 1920, Walterino Omiccioli followed his older brother Enzo's example and joined the *Regia Aeronautica* – and like his sibling, he became an ace.

Following his training at Ghedi, Omiccioli 'junior' was assigned as a Sergente Pilota to 98ª *Squadriglia*, 7º *Gruppo*, 54º *Stormo* just as the unit switched from Breda Ba.88 twin-engined ground attack aircraft to C.200 fighters. By then his brother had already been killed in combat in East Africa, losing his life on 3 February 1941 after claiming five victories – he received a posthumous Gold Medal for Military Valour.

Walter scored his first victory when he downed a Hurricane over Malta on 30 June 1941, sharing the kill with his commander, Capitano Gostini. On 25 July he destroyed a second Hawker fighter, although this time it was credited as an individual victory. The following day he claimed yet another Hurricane while escorting naval vessels of the *Regia Marina*. Omiccioli continued to enjoy success over the next three months, claiming a further trio of Hurricanes. On 14 October he participated in a strafing attack on Luqa airfield, where a number of aircraft were destroyed on the ground.

Finally returning to Italy with his unit in June 1942, the ace's good fortune in combat saw him down a Blenheim near his base at Reggio Calabria on 4 December, the bomber being forced to ditch in the Mediterranean just off the southern Italian port. This whole episode was witnessed by a sizeable crowd, cited in *Bollettino di Guerra* n.551 and widely publicised in the national press.

Injured twice in non-combat-related crashes during the course of 1942, Omiccioli finally returned to 54º *Stormo* in early 1943, by which time his unit had re-equipped with C.202s in preparation for the Tunisian campaign. Sent to El Hamma in late March, 98º *Squadriglia's* next phase of combat remains poorly documented due to the loss of its combat records during the evacuation of North Africa. However, subsequent postwar research has confirmed that Omiccioli was credited with two more individual victories, raising his tally to nine. This figure is featured in the citation recommending his promotion to the grade of Aiutante di Battaglia due to his meritorious service.

Towards the end of the Battle for Tunisia, on 11 May, Omiccioli was captured and made prisoner, and after a series of adventures (which merit a book of their own) he managed to escape from the camp at Souk el Kemis and return home. Postwar, he remained active in the *Aeronautica Militare* until reaching retirement age.

Walter Omiccioli received a Silver Medal and three Bronze Medals for Military Valour, as well as an Iron Cross, Second Class. Today, he lives in Treviso, where he continues to ardently support, and preside over, the local section of the *Opera Nazionale Combattenti e Reduci* (National Military Veterans Movement).

HOME DEFENCE

Luigi Gorrini

Luigi Gorrini is the highest ranking Italian ace still alive today, and the only surviving fighter pilot awarded the Gold Medal for Military Valour. Born at Alseno, in the province of Piacenza, on 12 July 1917,

A group of pilots from 7° *Gruppo* pose at Caselle whilst undergoing conversion training onto the C.202 in late 1942. Third from the left is Tenente Enzo Lombardo (seven victories), and immediately to his left, sat in the foreground, is Sergente Maggiore Walter Omiccioli (nine victories). Finally, second from right is Maresciallo Carlo Magnaghi (eleven victories)

he developed a passion for motorcycles at a very early age. This was subsequently eclipsed by a desire to fly, and after gaining his wings he was posted as a Sergente Pilota to 85ª *Squadriglia*, 18º *Gruppo*, 3º *Stormo* in February 1939. Amazingly, Gorrini was to serve with this unit right through to the Armistice.

In the autumn of 1940 his CR.42-equipped *squadriglia* formed part of the CAI in Belgium, where he participated in a handful of fierce air battles over the English Channel. As with fellow 18º *Gruppo* ace Bordoni Bisleri, Gorrini scored all of his kills either in North Africa or during the defence of Italy.

Notwithstanding the obsolescence of his Fiat biplane fighter come 1941, he managed to shoot down a Beaufighter on 16 April and a Blenheim on 29 May. Gorrini then spent many months without seeing any enemy aircraft when his unit was given the job of providing fighter escort for naval convoys. He also flew standing patrols and ground attack missions during this period. Indeed, Gorrini did not score his next victory until January 1943, by which time his unit was flying the C.202 in the desperate defence of Tunisia. He claimed both a P-40 and a Spitfire prior to 18º *Gruppo* returning to Italy in late March 1943.

Initially grounded due to an irritating eye injury, Gorrini quickly made up for lost time in July and August 1943. Now flying a C.205V, and based at Cerveteri, north of Rome, the veteran fighter pilot claimed four B-17s, four P-38s and a Spitfire with the cannon-armed Macchi fighter. He was also credited with the destruction of a fifth P-38 and a B-24 whilst flying a C.202.

A highly experienced fighter pilot by the time he fought in defence of Italian skies, Sergente Luigi Gorrini is seen at Ciampino Sud in late 1941 with his C.200. He obtained 11 of his 19 kills in July-August 1943

During the engagement in which the Liberator was downed, on 13 August, Gorrini's aircraft was hit by defensive fire from the doomed bomber, forcing the Italian ace to take to his parachute. Such a string of victories earned him the following mention in dispatches on 30 August;

'Sergente Maggiore Luigi Gorrini da Alseno (Piacenza) of 3º *Stormo Caccia* has distinguished himself during the aerial battles of the 27th and 29th, during which he has shot down two four-engined bombers and a twin-engined fighter.'

On 31 August, during his last operational sortie with the *Regia Aeronautica*, he shot down a Spitfire, but he in turn had to perform an emergency landing.

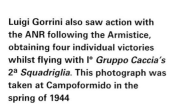

Luigi Gorrini also saw action with the ANR following the Armistice, obtaining four individual victories whilst flying with Iº *Gruppo Caccia's* 2ª *Squadriglia*. This photograph was taken at Campoformido in the spring of 1944

Gorrini suffered numerous injuries in the resulting crash, duly spending several weeks in hospital recuperating.

In the wake of the Armistice, he joined a large number of other fighter pilots who responded to an appeal launched by the famous 'Gamba di Ferro', Tenente Colonnello Ernesto Botto, to continue the fight on the side of the *Aeronautica Nazionale Repubblicana*. Assigned to I° *Gruppo Caccia's* 2ª *Squadriglia*, Gorrini used the C.205V to claim a further four victories between January and April 1944, bringing his tally to 19 – other unconfirmed sources credit him with as many as 24 victories. On 15 June, Gorrini was shot down for a second time, bringing his career as a fighter pilot to an end.

He remained in the air force after the war, being nominated Ufficiale on retirement. In 1958 he received the rare honour of being awarded the Gold Medal for Military Valour, this decoration usually only being bestowed posthumously. This was added to his previous two Bronze Medals and a German Iron Cross, Second Class. Today, Luigi Gorrini continues to live in the town of his birth, Alseno

RUSSIAN FRONT

Giuseppe Biron

Giuseppe 'Bepi' Biron was born in Legnago, in the province of Verona, on 12 October, 1914. In April 1933 he joined the *Regia Aeronautica* as a student Sergente Pilota and in September he received his military 'wings'. Initially assigned to 4° *Stormo*, Biron transferred to 108ª *Squadriglia Osservazione Aerea* in East Africa, although he was invalided back to Italy due to ill health prior to completing his tour.

Following a short spell with 6° *Stormo*, Biron volunteered for service in Spain, flying firstly with 33ª *Squadriglia* of VI° *Gruppo* 'Gamba di Ferro' and then the 'Cucaracha'. Upon his return from Spain, Biron subsequently enrolled in a course to become a commissioned officer in December 1939, and in May 1941 he was appointed Sottotenente. He then joined 22° *Gruppo Autonomo's* 369ª *Squadriglia* (equipped with C.200s) just as it was preparing to leave for the Russian Front.

One of the leading fighter pilots during the Russian campaign was Sottotenente 'Bepi' Biron, who is seen here alongside the emblem he designed for 22° *Gruppo Autonomo*

On the way to the Ukraine, the *gruppo* landed at Tirana to refuel its Macchi fighters, and it was whilst here that Biron, inspired by the emblem of the 'Cucaracha' (a cockroach playing a saxophone, from which have 'sprouted' a number of small red aircraft), sketched within a similar triangle a scarecrow smoking a pipe, with red stars floating in its smoke.

The enemy fighters (I-16s) initially encountered by the Italians in the USSR were identical to those that had opposed them in Spain, and the emblem, which

brought back memories of the *Aviación Legionaria's* victorious days, was adopted for good luck. Worn by the *gruppo's* C.200s, the marking survived the war to be carried by Starfighters of the Italian Air Force.

Once in-theatre the pilots of 22° *Gruppo* found themselves operating in appalling conditions, with the open cockpits of their C.200s proving particularly unsuited to the freezing weather of the Russian winter. Notwithstanding such difficulties, Biron displayed his undoubted flying skill during February and March 1942 by sharing in the destruction of a number of I-16s and MiG-3s. Unfortunately, the official records for 22° *Gruppo's* operations in Russia do not record individual victories, although careful analysis of combat reports indicate that at least four aircraft (other sources claim six) can be attributed to Sottotenente Biron.

Posted away from the Eastern Front in the spring of 1942, 22° *Gruppo* was duly committed to the aerial defence of southern Italy, and between 21 and 28 August 1943 Biron was credited with the destruction of a B-17 and three P-38s. By this time individual victories were being officially recorded at unit level, with successful pilots receiving financial rewards – the level of the 'pay out' varied according to whether the aircraft destroyed was single-, twin- or multi-engined!

Following the Armistice Biron chose to side with the RSI, joining the *Squadriglia Complementare Montefusco-Bonet*, which was later integrated into I° *Gruppo Caccia* under the command of Maggiore Visconti. Like all other pilots who served in the ANR, he was expelled from the air force after the war, eventually being recalled for service in 1950 once allegations of his collaboration with the Germans had been dispelled. Giuseppe Biron left the service in 1971, having attained the rank of Colonello. His decorations include five Silver and two Bronze Medals for Military Valour and an Iron Cross, Second Class. Alive and well as this volume went to press, he lives in Treviso.

AERONAUTICA NAZIONALE REPUBBLICANA

Adriano Visconti

Adriano Visconti became the figurehead of the *Aeronautica Nazionale Repubblicana* (ANR) mainly due to his charismatic command style and record as an able, courageous pilot.

He was born in Tripoli on 11 November 1915 to a family of noble origins, his father, Galeazzo, having served in the North African colonialisation expedition of 1911, where he remained in search of his fortune. Young Adriano grew up in a family environment charged with patriotic sentiment, and this sense of duty to Italy was to strongly influence all of his future career decisions. On completing his higher studies he applied to join the *Accademia Aeronautica*, where he was enrolled in the 'Rex' course.

In 1939 Visconti was commissioned as a Sottotenente Pilota and assigned to an 'assault' (ground attack) unit. This took the form of 159ª *Squadriglia* (12° *Gruppo*, 50° *Stormo*), based at Tobruk, which was equipped with the Breda Ba.65. He was then posted briefly to 2° *Gruppo Aviazione Presidio Coloniale's* 23ª *Squadriglia* for disciplinary reasons, but was allowed to return to his original unit following a display of heroism under fire which also earned him a Bronze Medal. The action in question had occurred when Visconti was attacked by three Gladiators from No 33 Sqn whilst flying a Ca.309 Ghibli reconnaissance aircraft. Thanks to his exceptional skill as a pilot, he and his crew managed to escape with their lives.

Once back flying the Ba.65 with 159ª *Squadriglia*, he undertook an intense cycle of operations against British armoured units in the desert. 50º *Stormo* suffered such appalling losses with the vulnerable Bredas during this time that the unit was disbanded in January 1941, and Tenente Visconti found himself posted to Treviso-based 76ª *Squadriglia* (7º *Gruppo*, 54º *Stormo*). Now flying C.200s, Visconti had soon mastered the art of being a fighter pilot, and he went on to perform numerous bomber escort and aerial reconnaissance (in modified C.200s fitted with a photo-planometric camera) sorties over Malta

The employment of smaller, faster aircraft for the critical 'photo-recce' mission relieved the pressure on the S.79s and Z.1007s that had been tasked with these sorties up to then. And modified fighters quickly proved to be far less vulnerable to Malta's fighters than camera-toting bombers.

Early in 1942 a handful of faster C.202s took over this mission from the C.200, and Visconti was often assigned one of these rare aircraft when a photo-reconnaissance sortie over Malta was scheduled.

On 15 June 1942, during the Battle of Pantelleria, he scored his first victory whilst flying a C.202 when he downed a Blenheim, and he followed this up on 13 August with two Spitfires. After a spell in Greece, and subsequent re-equipment with the C.202, 54º *Stormo* was rushed to Tunisia in March 1943.

Visconti, who had by then been promoted to Capitano and appointed commander of 76ª *Squadriglia*, participated in numerous combat engagements during the bitter fighting to remain in North Africa. One such action took place on 8 April when he spotted a flight of three Spitfires whilst flying with his wingmen, Laiolo and Marconcini. The Italian pilots enjoyed both a height and positional advantage, so Visconti ordered the attack – all three individuals claimed victories after this one-sided engagement. He added a second Spitfire and a P-40 to his tally during the final days of the African campaign leading up to the Axis surrender on 13 May. Visconti was one of the few pilots to avoid capture, reaching Sicily in his C.202 along with his friend

Capitano Adriano Visconti boards his Bf 109G from Iº *Gruppo Caccia*, ANR, which he commanded through to the end of the war. Visconti, who fought from June 1940 through to April 1945, was instrumental in the formation of the *Aeronautica Nazionale Repubblicana*

Capitano Fioroni, whom he had also somehow managed to squeeze into the cockpit of his Macchi fighter.

Visconti was then placed in command of the newly-formed 310ª *Squadriglia Caccia Aerofotografica* (Aerial Photography Fighter Squadron) at Guidonia, due east of Rome. This unit performed high-speed armed reconnaissance with a handful of specially-modified C.205Vs, commencing operations in August. Flying the only aircraft capable of surviving a daylight 'photo-recce' mission over advancing allied forces, 310ª *Squadriglia* sent a detachment to Decimomannu in early September. On the 9th of that month, feeling abandoned and without orders following the Armistice, Visconti flew back to Guidonia with three airmen 'stuffed' in the rear fuselage of his 'Veltro'! A similar flight was performed by his wingmen, Laiolo and Saieva.

A supporter of the ANR, Visconti initially took command of 1ª *Squadriglia Caccia* and then the entire Iº *Gruppo 'Asso di Bastoni'*. Sporting the rank of Maggiore, he was credited with four kills (two P-38s and two P-47s) prior to his unit's final capitulation. Having negotiated an honourable surrender for Iº *Gruppo*, Visconti was murdered by partisans in Milan on 29 April 1945 – they also killed his adjutant, Sottotenente Stefanini. He was decorated with four Silver Medals (plus another two awarded by the RSI) and two Bronze Medals for Military Valour, and an Iron Cross, Second Class.

Adriano Visconti has been credited with as many as 26 kills in various publications over the years, although he personally never claimed more than ten victories.

Ugo Drago

Ugo Drago was born at Arborio (Vercelli) on 3 March 1915. He obtained a diploma from the Rome Accademia di Educazione Fisica (Academy of Physical Education), working for a time as an instructor before deciding to join the air force. He obtained his 'wings' in 1939, was given the temporary grade of Sottotenente, and was posted to CR.42-equipped 363ª *Squadriglia*, 150º *Gruppo*. He eventually rose to the position of commander of this unit in June 1942, and he remained with the *gruppo* up until the Armistice was announced.

Drago had obtained his first victory whilst flying a CR.42 on 2 November 1940, the future ace downing a Greek PZL P.11 during a bomber escort mission to Salonicco. Another two Polish-built fighters fell to his Safat guns on 14 November over Koritza, and he claimed a Blenheim on 13 February 1941. At the end of the Greek campaign, having re-equipped with C.200s, 150º *Gruppo* remained in the Balkans to defend the territory captured by the Axis powers. The unit stayed in Greece until December 1941, when it was posted to North Africa to undertake convoy escort and tactical support missions.

Starved of opportunities to add to his tally of four kills, Drago was transferred with the *gruppo* to Sicily in the spring of 1943, where it became the first unit in the *Regia Aeronautica* to re-equip with the Bf 109G. After initial teething troubles with the Messerschmitt fighter during the brief work-up period, the Italian pilots soon grew to appreciate the aircraft's proven operational capabilities.

On 9 June a signal from the Sicilian HQ of the *Regia Aeronautica* to the Air Ministry reported how that 14 C.202s and four Bf 109s had 'engaged a formation of some 50 Spitfires and P-38s in combat in the skies above Pantelleria – four Spitfires were shot down, plus four more probably destroyed'. During the course of the battle Drago and two other Italian pilots had been shot down. A second signal soon followed the first, reporting that 'Tenente Pilota Drago of the 150° *Gruppo*, who returned last night from Pantelleria in a S.81, has declared that he definitely shot down two Spitfires during the engagment over Pantelleria'. These would be his last kills with the *Regia Aeronautica*.

Together with a good number of pilots from his *gruppo*, Ugo Drago chose to side with the *Repubblica Sociale Italiana* following the Armistice, joining II° *Gruppo Caccia*. He was given command of 1ª (later renumbered 4ª) *Squadriglia*, which flew G.55s for a short time before converting onto the Bf 109G. Drago was credited with 11 personal victories during the period 24 June 1944 to 23 March 1945, and was duly promoted to the rank of Capitano. These victories consisted of four P-47s, two P-51s, a P-38, a B-24, a Boston, a B-26 and a B-25. By VE-Day, Drago and Capitano Mario Bellagambi had jointly become the highest-scoring aces of the ANR.

Ugo Drago flew over 400 combat missions during World War 2, being decorated with three Silver Medals for Military Valour (plus another awarded by the RSI), two War Crosses, and German Iron Crosses, First and Second Class.

Post-war, he emigrated to Argentina (where he was joined by other Italian aces such as Giuseppe Robetto and Adriano Mantelli) and found employment as a flight instructor. In 1953 Drago returned home to join Alitalia, and subsequently enjoyed a long career as a Comandante. He presently lives in Rome.

THE LIST OF ACES

When attempting to create a definitive record of all Italian fighter aces of World War 1, the historian can turn to the *'Lista Benvenuti'* which, although containing minor errors, gives a complete 'official' listing of all 42 aces of that conflict. However, no such document exists for World War 2. The table on pages' 86-87, therefore, reflects much personal research by the authors using Air Ministry archives, in conjunction with original documentation belonging to surviving pilots, or their families. Indeed, the facts gleaned from first-hand material (unit diaries, log books, etc.) have had a great influence on this list, being used instead of journalistic or secondary accounts which often prove to be unreliable, or at least unconfirmable.

Traditionally, some pilots have been credited with a markedly different final tally of kills (usually much higher) to that which we have presented here. This is due to the fact that our list includes only confirmed kills, and excludes shared victories. In some squadron diaries, shared claims were attributed to those pilots who were actually involved in the action, while in others, commanders credited such kills to all who took part in the mission, whether they fired their guns at the enemy or not! No account has been taken of 'probables' either.

Weighed down with all the accoutrements associated with a fighter pilot in the final months of the war, II° *Gruppo Caccia's* Capitano Ugo Drago stands on the wing of his Bf 109G

The following list features names (and associated scores) that have regularly appeared in previous publications dealing with Italian aces. These individuals do not, however, feature in our list;

Col Mario Bonzano	15
Ten Col Duilio Fanali	15
Ten Giovanni Dell'Innocenti	12
Ten Furio Lauri	11
Magg Pietro Serini	11
Serg Magg Giov Batt Ceoletta	10+
Magg Angelo Mastragostino	10
Ten Angelo Fornoncini	9
Serg Magg Filippo Guarnaccia	7
Cap Germano La Ferla	6
Ten Gian Mario Zuccarini	6
Cap Livio Ceccotti	5
M llo Giuseppe Chiussi	5
S Ten Ezio Dell'Acqua	5
Serg M Antonio Franciosi	5
S Ten Remo Lugari	5
Terg Magg Lorenzo Migliorato	5
Ten Giorgio Oberweger	5
Serg Giampiero Svanini	5
Cap Salvatore Teja	5
Ten Col Antonio Vizzotto	5

Following much research into these pilots, we can confirm that some of the tallies resulted from the misinterpretation of official documentation. For example, Maggiore Pietro Serini has been credited with all the kills claimed by his unit, while the scores of Tenente Dell'Innocenti and Fornoncini include aircraft which were only damaged. And although some of the other tallies could be correct, we have failed to discover documentation confirming these kills.

Despite their removal from our listing, it should be pointed out, however, that three of these pilots (Lauri, Ceccotti and Serini) were decorated with the Gold Medal for Military Valour.

Aside from those names listed above, other published sources have also accorded Capitano Vasco Magrini (11 victories) and Maresciallo Ademade Angelotti (12) with ace status, when they never actaully belonged to a combat unit in World War 2!

Despite our research, we must still acknowledge the fact that the listing of aces presented here is not definitive. Indeed, it is highly unlikely that such a thing will ever exist, for much documentation (including virtually all the unit diaries relating to 1943, together with many log books) was either lost during the war, or in the 55 years since VE-Day.

One final note. A campaign description and pilot biographies for the Italian aces unique to the Spanish Civil War have not been included due to the fact that their exploits fall outside the scope of this book. However, Spanish kills scored by those pilots who went on to become aces in World War 2 are mentioned both in the full listing contained overleaf, and in the biographical entries that have preceded it.

ITALIAN ACES OF WORLD WAR 2

rank	name	claims	units	decorations.	kia/mia
serg m	Teresio Martinoli	22	384ª, 78ª, 84ª, 73ª	o, 2a, Ek2	25/8/44
cap	Franco Lucchini	21 (+1 Spain)	90ª, c 84ª, c 10° Gr	o, 5a, b, 3c, Ek2	5/7/43
s ten	Leonardo Ferrulli	20 (+1 Spain)	91ª, 90ª	o, 3a	5/7/43
ten	Franco Bordoni Bisleri	19	95ª, 85ª, 83ª	3a, Ek2	
m llo	Luigi Gorrini	19	85ª, 2ª ANR	o, 2b, Ek1, 2	
cap	Ugo Drago	17	363ª, c 4ª ANR	3a, c, Ek1, 2	
cap	Mario Visintini	16 (+1 Spain)	412a	o, a, b	11/2/41
magg	Mario Bellagambi	14	354ª, c 364ª, c 5ª ANR	3a, Ek1, 2	
serg m	Luigi Baron	12	412ª	a, b, Ek2	
cap	Luigi Giannella	12	92ª, c 84ª	3a	
serg m	Attilio Sanson	12	362ª, 5ª ANR	2a, b, Ek2	
m llo	Carlo Magnaghi	11	76ª, 98ª, 310ª, 1ª ANR	2a, 3b, Ek2	13/5/44
cap	Giorgio Solaroli di Briona	11	74ª, 377ª, c 95ª	2a, b, Ek2	
serg m	Mario Veronesi	11	84ª, 1ª ANR	a, b, Ek2	
m llo	Amedeo Benati	10	77ª, 79ª, 3ª ANR	a, b	
cap	Fernando Malvezzi	10	236ª, c 97ª, c III° Gr ANR	3a, b, Ek2	
cap	Giulio Reiner	10	c 73ª	a, b, Ek2	
cap	Giuseppe Robetto	10	167ª, 76ª, 86ª, 1ª ANR	a, b, Ek1, 2	
magg	Carlo Maurizio Ruspoli di Poggio Suasa	10	81ª, c 91ª	3a, Ek2	
serg m	Massimo Salvatore	10	90ª	a, 4b	
cap	Claudio Solaro	10 (+1 Spain)	c 70ª	2a, 3b, Ek2	
m llo	Ennio Tarantola	10 (+1 Spain)	239ª, 151ª, M-B ANR	4a, 2b	
cap	Giulio Torresi	10	77ª, 362ª, c 3ª ANR	4a, Ek2	1/7/44
magg	Adriano Visconti	10	159ª, c 76ª, c 310ª, c I° Gr ANR	4a, 2b, Ek1	29/4/45
cap	Emanuele Annoni	9	c 96ª	3a, b	
ten	Giovanni Barcaro	9	c 97ª, c 7ª ANR	2a	
serg m	Fausto Fornaci	9	362ª, 5ª ANR	a, b, 2c, Ek2	6/2/45
serg m	Walter Omiccioli	9	98ª	a, 3b, Ek2	
s ten	Natalino Stabile	9 (+1 Spain)	88ª, 3ª ANR	a, b, Ek2	
ten	Giuseppe Biron	8	369ª, M-B ANR	5a, 2b, Ek2	
cap	Giovanni Bonet	8	70ª, 359ª, c 150ª, c M-B ANR	4a, Ek2	29/3/44
s ten	Antonio Camaioni	8	395ª, 363ª, 6ª ANR	a, b	
ten	Fausto Filippi	8	363ª, 5ª ANR	a, Ek2	23/1/45
ten	Antonio Longhini	8	370ª, 355ª, 2ª ANR	2a, 2b	16/11/44
ten	Orfeo Mazzitelli	8	359ª, 371ª	b	
m llo	Aroldo Soffritti	8	412ª	2a	
ten	Raffaele Valenzano	8	370ª, 78ª, 372ª, 4ª ANR	a, Ek2	
cap	Tito Valtancoli	8	373ª, 86ª, c 375ª	a	
serg	Bruno Biagini	7	96ª	a, 2b	
ten	Carlo Canella	7	412ª	2a, b	
ten	Antonio Canfora	7	97ª	2a	
s ten	Agostino Celentano	7	150ª, M-B ANR	2a	
ten	Vittorino Daffara	7 (+3 Spain)	81ª, 97ª	5a, b	
magg	Luigi Filippi	7	75ª, c 156° Gr, c 23° Gr	3a, bva	20/2/43
m llo	Dino Forlani	7	79ª, 2ª ANR	a, b, c, Ek2	
t col	Ettore Foschini	7 (+1 Spain)	c 355ª, c 21° Gr	3a, 2b, Ek2	
m llo	Roberto Gaucci	7	360ª, 378ª	4a, b, c	
ten	Enzo Lombardo Schiappacasse	7	98ª	a, b	
ten	Orlando Mandolini	7	93ª, 91ª	a, c, Ek2	
ten	Mario Mecatti	7	364ª, 91ª	a, b, c	
magg	Carlo Miani	7 (+1 Spain)	c 360ª, c II° Gr ANR	4a,2b,Ek2	
magg	Furio Niclot Doglio	7	353ª, c 151ª	o, a, 2b, ava, Ek2	27/7/42
cap	Clizio Nioi	7	c 80ª	3a	
ten	Giuseppe Oblach	7	73ª	o, 2a	1/12/42
cap	Ranieri Piccolomini Clementini	7	97ª, c 90ª, c 10° Gr	3a, 2b	
m llo	Angelo Savini	7	90ª	a, 2b	
serg	Ferruccio Serafini	7	378ª	o, a	22/7/43
ten	Virgilio Vanzan	7	82ª, 90ª	2a	
ten	Osvaldo Bartolozzi	6	300ª, 413ª	2a, b	
m llo	GianLino Baschirotto	6 (+5 Spain)	88ª	4a, b, Ek2	
ten	Livio Bassi	6	395ª, 361ª	o	2/4/41
cap	Piero Bonfatti	6	c 73ª	2a, b	22/11/41
m llo	Aldo Buvoli	6 (+2 Spain)	360ª, 378ª	3a, b, c	
s ten	Carlo Cucchi	6	385ª, 1ª ANR	a	
s ten	Rinaldo Damiani	6	97ª	2b	

serg m	Cesare Di Bert	6	150ª	a	
m llo	Guido Fibbia	6 (+3 Spain)	365ª, 95ª, 2ª ANR	2a, b, c, Ek2	
ten	Giuliano Fissore	6	395ª, 393ª, 360ª, 6ª ANR	3a	
cap	Amedeo Guidi	6	c 366ª, c 2ª ANR	a, 2c	
serg m	Domenico Laiolo	6	76ª, 363ª, 310ª, 1ª ANR	a, c, Ek2	
serg m	Giuseppe Marconcini	6	76ª, 310ª, 1ª ANR	a, Ek2	
cap	Sergio Maurer	6	c 98ª	2a, b, c	6/5/43
s ten	Alvaro Querci	6	73ª, 96ª	2a, bva	
serg	Diego Rodoz	6	167ª, 1ª ANR	a, b	
cap	Alberto Spigaglia	6	364ª, II° Gr ANR	2a, b, c	
ten	Vittorio Squarcia	6	73ª	2a	
ten	Alberto Veronese	6	410ª, 303ª	2a	4/11/44
serg m	Loris Baldi	5	396ª, 4ª ANR	-	
s ten	Luigi Bandini	5	70ª, 153ª, 95ª, 2ª ANR	a	29/4/44
serg	Lucio Biagini	5	359ª, 2ª ANR	3a, c	25/4/44
serg	Manfredo Bianchi	5	395ª	a	
m llo	Pietro Bianchi	5	352ª	o, 2a, b, 2c	2/8/43
m llo	Alessandro Bladelli	5	91ª	2a, 2b	
s ten	Evasio Cavalli	5	355ª	a	21/7/43
cap	Guglielmo Chiarini	5	82ª, 366ª, 368ª	o, 2a, 2b, c	4/2/41
m llo	Tullio Covre	5	353ª, 86ª, 5ª ANR	a, ava	
serg	Francesco Cuscunà	5	75ª, 2ª ANR	2a	
serg m	Facchini Dotta	5	169ª	2a, c	
serg m	Domenico Ettore	5	78ª, 76ª, 363ª, 1ª ANR	a, 3b	
ten	Giuseppe Ferrazani	5	356ª, 160ª, 90ª	a, b	
ten	Iacopo Frigerio	5	97ª	3a, b, c, ova	
serg m	Antonio Giardinà	5	410ª, 300ª	2a, b	
cap	Eber Giudice	5	393ª, 352ª, 164ª, c 371ª	a, b, bva	
cap	Giorgio Graffer	5	c 365ª	o, b	28/11/40
serg	Mario Guerci	5	73ª	2a, b	
serg m	Spiridione Guiducci	5	353ª, 357ª	b, 2c	
m llo	Felice Longhi	5 (+1 Spain)	95ª	3a, c, Ek2	
magg	Luigi Mariotti	5	363ª, 91ª, c 9° Gr	o, 4a, b	27/12/44
ten	Mario Melis	5	352ª, 85ª	2a	12/5/44
magg	Vittorio Minguzzi	5	359ª, c 22° Gr	4a, b	
s ten	Elio Miotto	5	91ª	3a	21/3/45
ten	Gianfranco Montagnani	5	352ª, 359ª	4a, Ek2	7/9/42
serg m	Amleto Monterumici	5	90ª	a, b, 2c	
ten	Enrico Moretto	5	96ª, 370ª	a	19/1/43
m llo	Luigi Morosi	5	81ª, 3ª ANR	3a, Ek2	6/4/44
cap	Dante Ocarso	5	c 88ª	3a, Ek2	28/11/42
serg m	Enzo Omiccioli	5	410ª, 412ª	o, a	3/2/41
ten	Antonio Palazzeschi	5	81ª	2a, Ek2	
m llo	Francesco Pecchiari	5	352ª	2a, 2c	6/7/42
serg m	Luciano Perdoni	5	84ª	a, 2b, 3c	
ten	Costantino Petrosellini	5	92ª	a	
cap	Mario Pinna	5	70ª, 75ª, c 74ª	2a, b	
ten	Giorgio Pocek	5	354ª, 150ª	3a, c	
magg	Riccardo Roveda	5	c 353ª	2a, b, Ek2	
s ten	Giovanni Sajeva	5	310ª, 1ª ANR	-	
magg	Pier Giuseppe Scarpetta	5 (+1 Spain)	c 360ª, c 150ª, c 98v, c 7° Gr	3a, 2b	14/8/42
ten	Carlo Seganti	5	239ª, 358ª	o, 2b	12/7/42
m llo	Olindo Simionato	5 (+1 Spain)	150ª	2a, 2b, Ek2	
cap	Annibale Sterzi	5 (+1 Spain)	c 358ª	o, 2a	26/5/42
ten	Renato Talamini	5	80ª, 3ª ANR	a, b	10/4/44
ten	Luigi Torchio	5	75ª, 377ª, 3ª ANR	a, c	30/1/44
magg	Giorgio Tugnoli	5 (+1 Spain)	c 153ª, c 74ª, c 23° Gr	3a, 3b	
serg m	Celso Zemella	5	70ª	3a, b, Ek2	

Key
c – Commanding Officer
Gr – Gruppo (Regia Aeronautica)
ANR – Aeronautica Nazionale Repubblicana
M-B – Montefusco-Bonet Squadriglia
o, a, b – medaglia d'oro, d'argento, di bronzo al valor militare (in decorations column)
c – croce di guerra al valor militare
ova, ava, bva – medaglia d'oro, d'argento, di bronzo al valor aeronautico (in decorations column)
Ek1 and Ek2 – German Iron Cross, first and second class (in decorations column)

APPENDICES

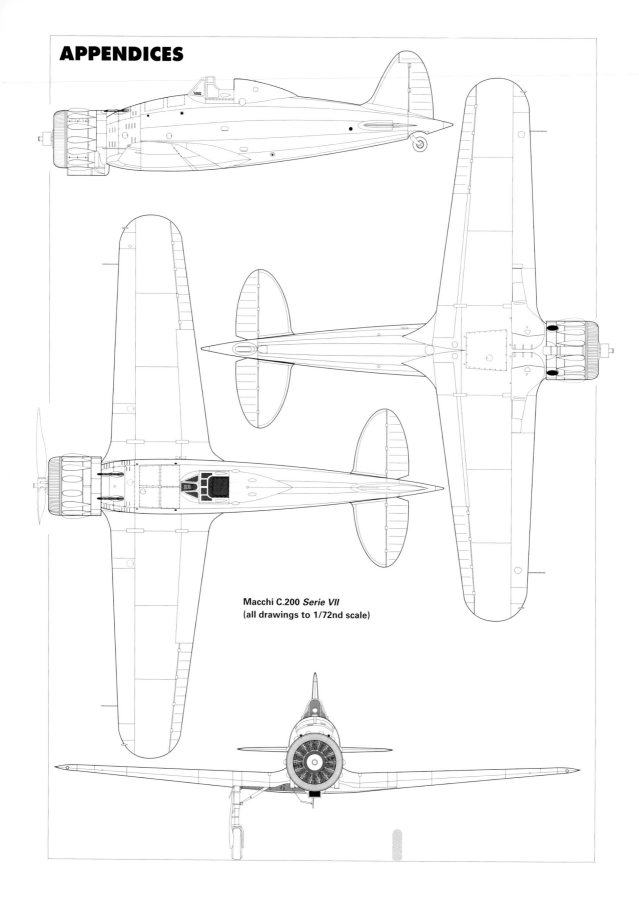

Macchi C.200 *Serie VII*
(all drawings to 1/72nd scale)

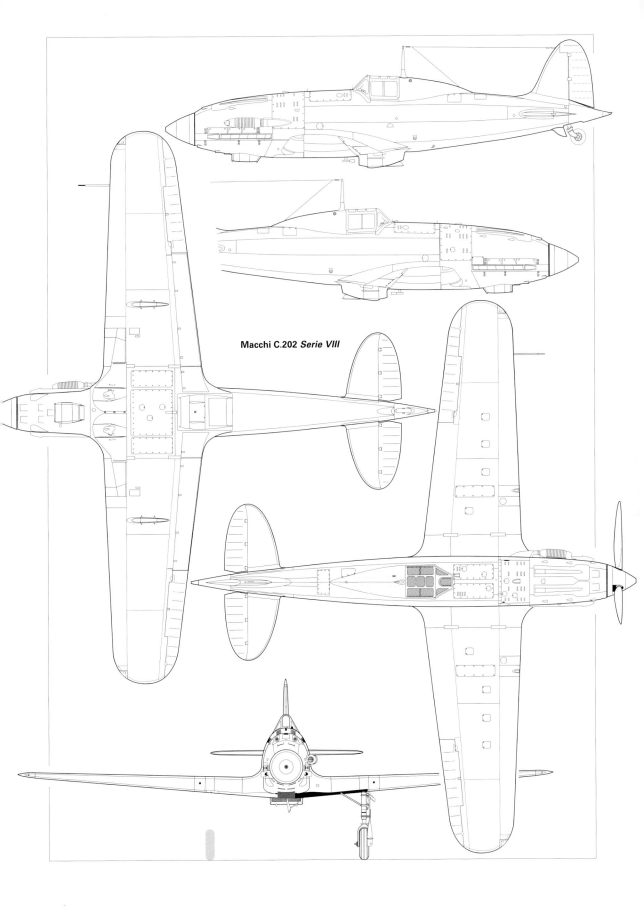

Macchi C.202 *Serie VIII*

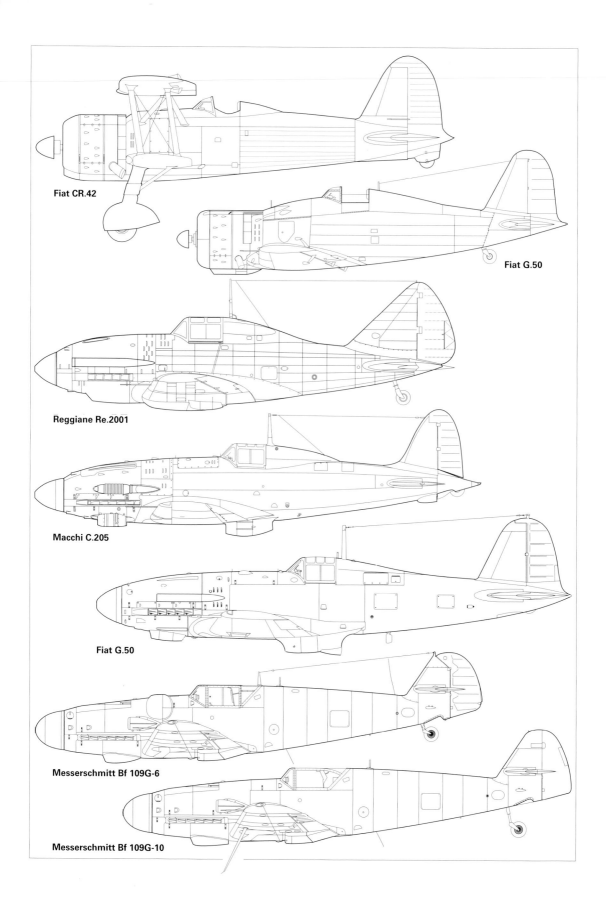

Fiat CR.42

Fiat G.50

Reggiane Re.2001

Macchi C.205

Fiat G.50

Messerschmitt Bf 109G-6

Messerschmitt Bf 109G-10

COLOUR PLATES

1

CR.42 of Capitano Giorgio Graffer, CO of 365ª *Squadriglia*, 150° *Gruppo*, 53° *Stormo*, Caselle, summer 1940

This Fiat fighter is finished in the classic three-tone camouflage of the period – Verde (green), Marrone (brown) and Giallo Mimetico (yellow). Capitano Graffer was flying a CR.42 devoid of a radio and specialist nightfighter equipment when he successfully intercepted an RAF Whitley bomber over Turin on the night of 13/14 August 1940.

2

CR.42 of Tenente Mario Visintini, 412ª *Squadriglia Autonoma*, Gura, summer 1940

Again camouflaged in the standard three-tone scheme, this CR.42 lacks any specific East African theatre markings apart from the unit badge, which depicts a red prancing horse superimposed over a black map of Africa. This motif reflected the fact that many of the pilots within 412ª *Squadriglia* came from 4° *Stormo*. The individual number worn by Visintini's CR.42 is the result of an educated guess on the part of the authors, as none of the photographs of his aircraft that have so far come to light show this area of the fuselage.

3

CR.42 of Sottotenente Franco Bordoni Bisleri, 95ª *Squadriglia*, 18° *Gruppo*, 3° *Stormo*, Mirafiori, Summer 1940

The white spinner of Bisleri's fighter signified that it belonged to 95ª *Squadriglia* – 83ª and 85ª*Squadriglia* used red and green spinners respectively). In a rare early-war example of aircraft individualisation within the *Regia Aeronautica*, the ace had the word *ROBUR* painted on his fighter's headrest fairing in white. This was Bisleri's nickname, and it was derived from the advertising slogan of a famous liqueur produced by his family firm. Bisleri claimed five kills with the CR.42 in North Africa.

4

CR.42 of Maresciallo Felice Longhi, 95ª *Squadriglia*, 18° *Gruppo*, 3° *Stormo*, Mirafiori, Summer 1940

Longhi's CR.42 was a virtual mirror image of Bisleri's fighter, the two pilots often participating in the same missions during this early stage of the war in the west. The 18° *Gruppo* 'Ocio che te copo' emblem is derived from the badge used by *Squadriglia Mitragliamento* ('strafing squadron') *'Frecce'* of the Spanish war – Longhi had downed an I-15 while flying the CR.32 in the latter conflict. He used this particular CR.42 to shoot down a Blenheim in North Africa in 1941, followed by three kills with the C.202 and one with the C.205V.

5

C.200 of Sottotenente Franco Bordoni Bisleri, 95ª *Squadriglia*, 18° *Gruppo*, 3° *Stormo*, Atene-Tatoi, October 1941

This C.200 is painted in the standard metropolitano (home front) scheme of Verde Oliva (Olive Green), the white fuselage band being applied to all Italian aircraft in November 1940. Received as a replacement for his CR.42 in the autumn of 1941, this C.200 was immediately personalised by Bordoni Bisleri. The ace failed to achieve any kills with this type.

6

C.200 of Tenente Franco Lucchini, 90ª *Squadriglia*, 10° *Gruppo*, 4° *Stormo*, Catania, August 1941

Lucchini's C.200 is seen in a typical *Regia Aeronautica* scheme of Giallo and Marrone Mimetico (yellow and brown) mottles over a Verde Mimetico (green) base. Most Macchi fighters wore this camouflage scheme during the spring-summer of 1941. The small red elephant painted beneath the cockpit was unique to aircraft of 90ª *Squadriglia*, whilst the prancing horse emblem belonged to 10° *Gruppo*. *Squadriglia* markings were abolished from all 4° *Stormo* aircraft during the course of 1942, and the Giallo Cromo (chrome yellow) engine cowling became standard throughout the *Regia Aeronautica* between March and October 1941. Lucchini claimed four victories in the C.200 over Malta between June and September 1941.

7

C.200 of Sottotenente Giuseppe Biron, 369ª *Squadriglia*, 22° *Gruppo Autonomo*, Krivoj-Rog, September 1941

Flown by one of the most successful Italian pilots to see action on the Eastern Front, this C.200 is camouflaged in a two-tone scheme. It also features the yellow fuselage band and underside wingtips that were adopted as theatre markings to facilitate rapid recognition by fellow Axis pilots, and friendly troops on the ground. The unique 'scarecrow smoking red stars' marking was adopted by 22° *Gruppo* as its emblem at Tirana prior to the unit arriving in Russia, the icon being created by Guiseppe Biron. Aside from achieving at least four individual kills in the USSR, Biron claimed a quartet of victories in August 1943 whilst flying a C.202 during the defence of Italy.

8

C.200 of Maggiore Ettore Foschini, CO of 21° *Gruppo Autonomo*, Stalino, May 1942

Painted in a three-tone densely mottled scheme, this aircraft features a tail cross with spans of equal length – typical of the C.200s built under licence by Breda. The Roman numerals and rank pennant on the fuselage band indicate that the fighter was flown by the *Gruppo* Commander, Ettore Foschini. A veteran of the Spanish war (where he claimed one kill), Foschini scored five victories in Greece with the CR.42 whilst leading 24° *Gruppo's* 355ª *Squadriglia*, followed by two kills in Russia with the C.200.

9

C.202 *Serie II* MM7712 of Sottotenente Jacopo Frigerio, 97ª *Squadriglia*, 9° *Gruppo*, 4° *Stormo*, Comiso, 30 September 1941

MM7712 was one of the first C.202s built by Aermacchi (it bore construction number 4), and it was painted in a scheme much favoured by the Varese-based firm – superimposed mottling of Giallo and Marrone Mimetico over Verde Mimetico, with a yellow nose area as per official directives. This aircraft is adorned with the two unit markings then worn by all 9° *Gruppo* fighters, namely the 'Cavallino Rampante' in white on a black shield on the fuselage and the 'Gamba di

Ferro' (iron leg) on the fin. Frigerio first flew MM7712 on 30 June 1941 when he ferried the fighter from Lonate Pozzolo to Gorizia. Upon moving to Comiso on 29 September, Frigerio claimed the type's very first victory (in this aircraft) the following day when he downed Hurricane II Z5265 of No 185 Sqn during a raid on the *gruppo's* new home. The fighter crashed off the Sicilian coast, and although its pilot (Plt Off D W Lintern) bailed out, he was never found. MM7712, which was later fitted with cameras, enjoyed a long career as a reconnaissance aircraft, serving with 54° *Stormo* (and flown by Adriano Visconti) and 377ª *Squadriglia Autonoma* (where it was used by another ace, Luigi Torchio) at Palermo.

10

C.202 *Serie III* MM7742 of Tenente Emanuele Annoni, 96ª *Squadriglia*, 9° *Gruppo*, 4° *Stormo*, Comiso, 14 October 1941

Near identical to MM7712, this aircraft wears the codes of fellow 9° *Gruppo* unit 96ª *Squadriglia,* which was also based at Comiso in the autumn on 1941. Nine-kill ace Annoni had to nurse this fighter back to base on 14 October 1941 after it was struck by two cannon shells fired by the No 185 Sqn Hurricane II flown by five-kill ace Plt Off David Barnwell. Malta's leading nightfighter pilot, Barnwell was in turn shot down and killed moments later by a second 96ª *Squadriglia* C.202. MM7742 was subsequently repaired over a number of months and assigned to 54° *Stormo* in April 1942.

11

C.202 *Serie III* MM7720 of Capitano Franco Lucchini, CO of 84ª *Squadriglia*, 10° *Gruppo*, 4° *Stormo*, Fuka, September 1942

This aircraft had originally served with 1° *Stormo* in an overall Verde Scuro scheme, although it was later repainted with large patches of Giallo Mimetico to render it less visible against the desert environment of North Africa. By this stage in its long career, the fighter had had its starboard wing replaced by a flying surface from a later C.202, which was painted in standard 'smoke ring' mottles of Verde Oliva over Nocciola Chiaro (light chestnut). The emblem worn on the fuselage stripe belonged to 10° *Gruppo*, while the stylised signature of Francesco Baracca (Italy's 'ace of aces' during World War1) adorned the noses of all 4° *Stormo* C.202s from the end of March 1942 onwards. Assigned to 84ª *Squadriglia* in early September 1942, MM7720 was almost certainly used by Capitano Lucchini during the numerous combat missions he flew as part of the El Alamein campaign. He also saw action at the controls of several other C.202s during this period, including MM7919 '84-12', which he crash-landed on 24 October 1942 following combat.

12

C.202 *Serie III* MM7764 of Sergente Maggiore Teresio Martinoli, 73ª *Squadriglia*, 9° *Gruppo*, 4° *Stormo*, Gela, July 1942

Originally delivered to 1° *Stormo*, this aircraft was transferred to 73ª *Squadriglia* at the end of June 1942. Painted in the regulation scheme specified for operations in the 'colonies', the C.202's overall base colour is Giallo Mimetico, with Verde Mimetico mottling. Its nose and wingtips have been marked in white, which was the standard recognition colour for the North African theatre. By this stage of the war 9° *Gruppo's* white horse emblem had been repositioned on the white fuselage band, while the 'Gamba di Ferro' had been eliminated from the fin altogether. Martinoli also frequently used other C.202s whilst in North Africa (including '73-7', which was usually flown by fellow ace Giulio Reiner), depending on the serviceablity of his own 'personal' aircraft.

13

G.50bis of Sergente Maggiore Aldo Buvoli, 378ª *Squadriglia*, 155° *Gruppo Autonomo*, Castel Benito, 9 July 1941

Featuring a yellow engine cowling, which was synonymous with this period (March-October 1941), Buvoli's Fiat is painted in a mixed camouflage scheme of Verde and Giallo Mimetico. As with most G.50s, the white tail cross extends over its fin and rudder. Buvoli took-off alone in this aircraft on the evening of 9 July 1941 to patrol over Tripoli harbour, and duly intercepted seven Blenheims sent to attack shipping in the area. Diving on the bombers as they performed a low-level attack on the port, he chased the formation out to sea, firing at each one of them in sequence. Buvoli was subsequently credited with four kills, No 110 Sqn reporting the loss of a similar number of Blenheim IVs on its very first mission since arriving in Malta from the UK in early July.

14

Re.2001 of Tenente Agostino Celentano, 150ª *Squadriglia*, 2° *Gruppo Autonomo*, San Pietro di Caltagirone, May 1942

As with most Re.2001s, this aircraft is painted Verde Oliva Scuro (dark olive green) overall, with Grigio Azzurro Chiaro (light blue grey) undersides. Enjoying more success than most with the Reggiane fighter, Celentano was credited with six victories over Malta – his only other kill was claimed in North Africa the previous year whilst flying a G.50.

15

C.200 of Tenente Costantino Petrosellini, 92ª *Squadriglia*, 8° *Gruppo*, 2° *Stormo*, Sarzana, August 1943

This C.200 again exhibits the standard home front scheme of dark olive green upper surfaces and light blue grey undersides. In accordance with instructions issued by the Air Ministry on 29 July 1943, all fasces markings were removed following the fall of Mussolini's government on 25 July. Petrosellini claimed four of his five victories whilst flying this aircraft, with the most significant of these being the B-17 which he forced down into the sea off the Tyrrenian coast on 3 September 1943. This was not only one of the last kills claimed by the *Regia Aeronautica*, but almost certainly the last for the C.200.

16

CR.42 of Tenente Luigi Torchio, 377ª *Squadriglia Autonoma*, Palermo, February 1943

Although painted black overall for night operations, this aircraft inexplicably retained its white fuselage band – this was usually painted out on CR.42 nightfighters. The *squadriglia's* specialised mission is well reflected in its choice of unit emblem. The need for nightfighters had been all but ignored in Italy pre-war, and attempts to remedy this situation through the introduction of suitable aircraft, and training, only really came into effect during the final months of the conflict. Luigi Torchio was one of just a handful of Italian fighter pilots to achieve night kills, his first taking the form of a Wellington downed over Palermo whilst flying a CR.42 on the night of 21/22 February 1943. He was subsequently credited with three victories flying C.202 '377-1' and one in a C.200.

17

C.202 *Serie VII* MM9042 of Capitano Furio Niclot Doglio, CO of 151ª *Squadriglia*, 20° *Gruppo*, 51° *Stormo*, Gela, 27 July 1942

This aircraft is painted in a scheme devised by Aermacchi for 'colonial' use, featuring Nocciola Chiaro (light chestnut) and Verde Oliva Scuro (dark olive green) upper surfaces. This camouflage pattern had been introduced from the spring of 1942, the company applying a base coat of light chestnut to all upper surfaces, over which were sprayed irregular rings (sometimes referred to as 'smoke rings') of dark olive green. Propeller spinners on all Italian aircraft were invariably painted white during this period, although no official specifications were ever issued to confirm this. 51° *Stormo's* famous 'black cat and green mice' emblem was carried on the fuselage band, forward of which MM9042 also boasted a rare command pennant. This identified the pilot as being a *squadriglia* commander, and was applied in conjunction with the individual aircraft number '1'. This particular C.202 had a short operational life, being ferried from Aermacchi to Ciampino on 16 June 1942, before arriving at Gela on the 24th. It was shot down over Malta on 27 July by Canadian ace George 'Buzz' Beurling, Capitano Doglio being killed when the fighter blew up in mid-air. The latter had achieved six victories over Malta in just twelve days prior to his demise.

18

C.202 *Serie VII* MM9066 of Maresciallo Ennio Tarantola, 151ª *Squadriglia*, 20° *Gruppo*, 51° *Stormo*, Gela, September 1942

As with Capitano Doglio's '151-1', this aircraft sports Aermacchi's factory scheme of the period. Note that the 51° *Stormo* badge appears to be larger on MM9066, and that the pilot's personal marking only appeared on the cowling's starboard side. The exhortation *Dai Banana!* ('Go for it Banana') refers to Tarantola's nickname, which harked back to his days as a fruit vendor. MM9066 was the second '151-2' used by the ace over Malta, the first (MM9032) being lost on 14 August 1942 whilst being flown by Capitano Egeo Pittoni, who took to his parachute after the Macchi had been shot up by a No 1435 Sqn Spitfire V flown by future Canadian ace Flt Sgt Ian Maclennan. MM9066 features seven kill markings on its rudder, dating the profile to September 1942. At that time, Tarantola's tally included a P-40 shot down in North Africa, three personal Spitfire kills, plus two shared over Malta with Niclot, and a single I-15 from the ace's time in Spain (this marking was applied in red). Rarely seen on Italian fighters, victory symbols usually took the form of aircraft silhouettes.

19

C.202 *Serie VI* MM8339 of Capitano Carlo Miani, CO of 360ª *Squadriglia*, 155° *Gruppo*, 51° *Stormo*, Gela, August 1942

The very first *Serie VI* C.202, this Breda-built aircraft is camouflaged in the scheme favoured by the manufacturer – small, elongated Verde Oliva mottling over a Nocciola Chiaro base. Note the demarcation line between the camouflaged upper surfaces and the Grigio Azzurro Chiaro undersurfaces, the latter extending under the engine cowling, radiator and rear fuselage, rising up to the horizontal tail surfaces. A one-kill veteran of the Spanish war, future ace Carlo Miani downed three Spitfires over Malta in June 1942, although he was forced to abandon MM8339 and take to his parachute on 14 July due to chronic mechanical failure.

20

C.202 *Serie I* MM7944 of Tenente Adriano Visconti, 86ª *Squadriglia*, 7° *Gruppo*, 4° *Stormo*, Pantelleria, May 1942

Built in March 1942, and subsequently modified for photo-reconnaissance operations, MM7944 was initially assigned to 168ª *Squadriglia* (16° *Gruppo*, 54° *Stormo*), before being passed on to 7° *Gruppo* on 21 April. Although camouflaged in a typical Breda scheme, the fighter's 'Dare in Brocca' ('Hit with Precision') emblem was probably unique to MM7944. Visconti, who was assigned to 7° *Gruppo's* 76ª *Squadriglia*, frequently put his 'photo-recce' experience to good use at the controls of this machine. It is almost certain that he also used MM7944 to obtain his first victory (a Blenheim) during the Battle of Pantelleria on 15 June 1942.

21

C.202 *Serie III* MM7844 of Capitano Carlo Maurizio Ruspoli, CO of 91ª *Squadriglia*, 10° *Gruppo*, 4° *Stormo*, Fuka, September 1942

For much of World War 2, Prince Ruspoli flew aircraft equipped with ciné cameras, and C.202 '91-3' was no exception, boasting a small camera fitted in the leading edge of the starboard wing. Flown for the first time on 31 March 1942, MM7844 was painted in a scheme near-identical to that worn by Martinoli's '73-4' (profile 12), although in this instance Ruspoli's C.202 had the colours reversed – the mottling was applied in Nocciola Chiaro over a Verde Oliva Scuro base. The fighter's primer-coloured air filter denotes that this is a replacement item fitted 'in the field'.

22

C.202 *Serie III* MM7821 of Tenente Emanuele Annoni, CO of 96ª *Squadriglia*, 9° *Gruppo*, 4° *Stormo*, Fuka, 19 September 1942

From the same production batch as Ruspoli's aircraft, this C.202 has both a 9° *Gruppo* emblem on its fuselage band and a stylised *4° F Baracca* marking on its nose. Considered by Annoni to be both well trimmed and balanced, MM7821 was the ideal candidate to be 'loaned' to German ace Hans-Joachim Marseille on 19 September 1942 when he visited 4° *Stormo*. Although a brilliant fighter pilot, Marseille's limited knowledge of Italian aircraft was graphically revealed when he mistakenly cut the engine during his final approach to Fuka and was forced to belly-land the C.202.

23

C.202 *Serie I* MM7910 of Maresciallo Alessandro Bladelli, 91ª *Squadriglia*, 10° *Gruppo*, 4° *Stormo*, Fuka, September 1942

Compared with other 4° *Stormo* C.202s in North Africa at this time, MM7910 has only sparse mottling. Retiring as a general from the postwar Italian air force, Bladelli fought throughout World War 2 with 4° *Stormo*, achieving at least five personal victories in North Africa and sharing in three others. He was also credited with one of the few German aircraft downed after the Armistice, claiming a Ju 52/3m on 23 October 1943 in conjunction with fellow ace Tenente Giuseppe Ferrazani.

24

C.202 *Serie III* MM7944 of Tenente Giulio Reiner, CO of 73ª *Squadriglia*, 9° *Gruppo*, 4° *Stormo*, Fuka, August 1942

This aircraft features a scheme near identical to that applied to Carlo Rispoli's C.202 (profile 21). Note that MM7944 has white wingtips to denote its assignment to the North African theatre. Barely visible on its fin are two kill markings.

25

C.202 *Serie VII* MM9024(?) of Maggiore Luigi Filippi, CO of 23° *Gruppo*, 3° *Stormo*, Tunisia, January 1943

Filippi's C.202 displays an unusual version of the 'smoke ring' scheme that saw the elongated 'rings' connected to form an overall net pattern. The white '75' indicates the *squadriglia* to which the Macchi fighter belonged, while the fuselage pennant denotes the rank of its pilot. The 'Vespa Arrabiata' ('angry wasp') emblem was adopted by 3° *Stormo* when the previously autonomous 18° and 23° *Gruppi* merged in 1942.

26

C.202 *Serie III* of Sergente Maggiore Luigi Gorrini, 85ª *Squadriglia*, 18° *Gruppo*, 3° *Stormo*, Tunisia, January 1943

Wearing standard Aermacchi camouflage, this C.202 was transferred from 3° to 4° *Stormo* in November 1942. Luigi Gorrini frequently flew the aircraft in combat during the Italian retreat from Libya to Tunisia, shooting down a P-40 and a Spitfire with it in January 1943.

27

C.202 *Serie I* MM7913(?) of Tenente Giorgio Solaroli, CO of 74ª *Squadriglia*, 23° *Gruppo*, 3° *Stormo*, Tunisia, January 1943

Solaroli flew this aircraft when he assumed command of 74ª *Squadriglia*, scoring at least two victories with it in 1942. The fighter features a typical Breda colour scheme, with elongated patches of green mottling. 3° *Stormo's* emblem was carried on the white fuselage band, and for a short while aircraft from 74ª *Squadriglia* also had their individual number applied within a white triangle on the fin.

28

C.202 *Serie X* of Capitano Claudio Solaro, CO of 70ª *Squadriglia*, 23° *Gruppo*, 3° *Stormo*, Tunisia, January 1943

Near-identical to Solaroli's C.202, this aircraft does not carry the *gruppo* emblem, however. The units controlled by 3°*Stormo* each adopted their own style of numerical markings, and in the case of 70ª *Squadriglia*, its numbering was painted in outline only, with the individual aircraft number twice the size of the unit number. Solaro obtained his last victories in North Africa flying this particular C.202 – the ace claimed eight kills in less than three months in 1942-43.

29

C.202 *Serie III* of Sottotenente Leonardo Ferrulli, 91ª *Squadriglia*, 10° *Gruppo*, 4° *Stormo*, Fuka, October 1942

Ferrulli's C.202 is camouflaged in a standard Aermacchi scheme of small green mottles on a Nocciola Chiaro base – the latter shade may be Giallo Mimetico, which was a slightly lighter colour which replaced Nocciola Chiaro in the spring of 1942. Like many other aces of the North African campaign, Ferrulli flew a number of aircraft from this unit.

30

C.202 *Serie IX* of Sergente Maggiore Walter Omiccioli, 98ª *Squadriglia*, 7° *Gruppo*, 54° *Stormo*, Caselle, April 1943

This C.202 was built by Aermacchi and assigned to 7° *Gruppo* on the eve of its transfer to Tunisia – 54° *Stormo* became the last unit to leave African soil prior to the Axis surrender of 13 May 1943. Omiccioli scored his last two kills in Tunisia with this C.202, which bore his personal inscription, 'La Giulia longa ales i maron', on its starboard side.

31

C.202 *Serie X* MM9570 of Capitano Dante Ocarso, CO of 88ª *Squadriglia*, 6° *Gruppo*, 1° *Stormo*, Decimomannu, November 1942

Having claimed five P-40s in North Africa, Ocarso was to lose his life after ditching MM9570 in the Mediterranean in the wake of a strafing mission to Böne, on the Algerian coast, on 28 November 1942. Although he successfully vacated the fighter (which had only been delivered to the unit 18 days earlier), the ace had died from exposure by the time he was found adrift in his dinghy by fishermen ten days later.

32

C.202 *Serie IX* MM9398 of Marisciallo GianLino Baschirotto, 88ª *Squadriglia*, 6° *Gruppo*, 1° *Stormo*, Pantelleria, December 1942

This machine was delivered directly to 1° *Stormo's* Ciampino base from the Aermacchi factory on 13 November 1942, where it was adorned with the unit's distinctive 'Arciere' (archer) emblem and the motto 'Incocca tende scaglia' (a quote from Dannunzio). This C.202 was used by six-kill ace Baschirotto during the series of long-range missions flown by the unit over Algeria from bases in Sardinia, these sorties being performed in an effort to counter the *Torch* landings.

33

C.205V Veltro *Serie III* MM92156 of Sergente Ferruccio Serafini, 378ª *Squadriglia*, 155° *Gruppo Autonomo*, Capoterra, 22 July 1943

Aermacchi's characteristic C.202 camouflage scheme was also used on the Veltro, this particular machine being the fourth *Serie III* airframe completed. Following its delivery to 51° *Stormo* at Ciampino on 7 July 1943, MM92156 transferred to Sardinia with the unit. Seven-kill ace Serafini lost his life in this machine on 22 July during an engagement with P-40s from the 325th FG, although he succeeded in downing two of his opponents prior to his demise.

34

C.202 *Serie XI* of Tenente Orfeo Mazzitelli, 359ª *Squadriglia*, 22° *Gruppo Autonomo*, Capodichino, August 1943

Although this aircraft boasts a 'colonial' colour scheme, it was actually employed by 22° *Gruppo Autonomo* on home defence duties. Unlike other aircraft within this unit, this particular C.202 was not decorated with the 'scarecrow' emblem on its fuselage band. Eight-kill ace Mazzitelli achieved success with this fighter whilst defending Naples, downing six four-engined bombers during the course of 1943.

35

Bf 109G-6 Wk-Nr 18391 of Capitano Mario Bellagambi, CO of 364ª *Squadriglia*, 150° *Gruppo Autonomo*, Sciacca, June 1943

Delivered to the *Regia Aeronautica* in the spring of 1943, this aircraft is camouflaged in standard Luftwaffe colours of the period, namely RLM 74 and 75 upper surfaces, with mottles of the same colours over RLM 76 fuselage sides. The latter colour was also used for the undersurfaces, except for the yellow area beneath the engine cowling. Factory-applied German crosses were painted over with grey paint and replaced by Italian markings soon after the aircraft's arrival at Ciampino, although fuselage decals for the fasces, as well as the State emblem on the tail cross, were never applied. As with all other Bf 109s within this unit, the fighter wears the famous 150° *Gruppo Autonomo* 'Gigi Tre Osei' emblem within a white square ahead of its *squadriglia* number. Bellagambi flew numerous missions with this aircraft, sharing in the destruction of a B-24 on 30 June 1943. Wk-Nr 18391 was discovered by invading Allied forces in an unuseable condition at Sciacca just days later.

36

Bf 109G-6 Wk-Nr 18421 of Tenente Ugo Drago, CO of 363ª *Squadriglia*, 150° *Gruppo Autonomo*, Sciacca, June 1943

Although camouflaged near-identically to Bellagambi's Bf 109, this aircraft lacked the yellow theatre marking beneath its cowling. As with Bellagambi's *Gustav*, this fighter was found in a severely damaged state at Sciacca by the Allies. Most of Drago's fighters were marked with the number 7, and he ended the war flying Bf 109G-10 'Black 7' with II° *Gruppo Caccia*'s 4ª *Squadriglia*.

37

G.55 *Serie I* MM91065 probably flown by Capitano Giovanni Bonet, *Squadriglia Complementare Montefusco*, ANR, Venaria Reale, March 1944

One of the few units to use the G.55 operationally during World War 2, *Squadriglia Complementare Montefusco* (later *Montefusco Bonet*) experienced a short but intense campaign prior to merging with II° *Gruppo Caccia*. It features Verde Oliva Scuro upper surfaces and Grigio Azzurro Chiaro undersides. The new ANR markings adopted in January 1944 are also visible, these consisting of a tri-coloured flag bordered by yellow triangles. Wing markings (in this instance carried on the upper surfaces only) consisted of two black fasces, one facing forward and one rear, within a square black border. This aircraft had initially been operated by the Luftwaffe in the wake of the Italian Armistice of 8 September, the ANR having to crudely paint out the fuselage crosses and rudder swastikas following the fighter's return to their service in early 1944. Bonet had almost certainly flown this aircraft prior to his death on 29 March 1944 when, after claiming a

B-17, he was shot down by American ace 'Herky' Green of the 325th FG. Bonet had been credited with at least seven victories (some sources claim eleven) whilst flying with the *Regia Aeronautica* during the summer of 1943.

38

C.205V Veltro *Serie III* MM92287 of Capitano Adriano Visconti, CO of 1ª *Squadriglia*, I° *Gruppo Caccia*, ANR, Campoformido, April 1944

This ANR C.205V was camouflaged in a Luftwaffe-inspired scheme consisting of two greys for the upper surfaces and side mottling, with light blue-grey undersides. Its detail markings were also standard for the period – ANR flashes on the fuselage and fin, 1ª *Squadriglia* 'Asso di Bastoni' ('Ace of Clubs') emblem on the nose, and the unit number repeated on the main undercarriage doors. It was uncommon for pilots flying with I° *Gruppo Caccia* to be assigned personal aircraft, and apart from this machine, Visconti also flew '23-1' and '3-1', amongst others, during the early months of 1944.

39

Bf 109G-10/AS Wk-Nr 490379 of Maresciallo Attilio Sanson, 5ª *Squadriglia*, II° *Gruppo Caccia*, ANR, Osoppo, 3 March 1945

Camouflaged in standard Luftwaffe colours, this *Gustav* features the distinctive 'Diavolo Rosso' ('Red Devil') badge of 2ª (later 5ª) *Squadriglia*, commanded by Mario Bellagambi, on its nose. Again following German practice, a black spiral was introduced to the previously all white spinners of the Italian Bf 109Gs in July 1944. Aircraft of II° *Gruppo Caccia* normally carried dual national markings (except for the swastika). Maresciallo Sanson was wounded, and this Bf 109 written off, during an attack on USAAF bombers on 13 March 1945.

40

C.205V Veltro *Serie III* of Tenente Colonnello Duilio Fanali, CO of 155° *Gruppo*, Aeronautica Co-Belligerante, Lecce, late 1943

Even though Fanali does not appear in our list of aces (his log book only records two individual victories, apart from 33 shared kills during 1942 alone), his story certainly warrants inclusion. He commanded 155° *Gruppo* through to the Armistice, then led the *Aeronautica Co-Belligerante's* 51° *Stormo*. Post-war, he was head of the *Stato Maggiore* between 1968 and 1971. His C.205V was camouflaged in a typical 'smoke ring' scheme of the period, with heavy areas of retouching denoting the position of previous *Regia Aeronautica* markings – especially around the white fuselage band and the tail cross. The number '155' indicated the *gruppo* commanded by Fanali, while the arrow on the fighter's mainwheel cover (peculiar to this unit) indicated his grade of Maggiore – he was subsequently promoted to Tenente Colonnello due to his previous military service with the *Regia Aeronautica*. Although the propeller spinner colours are hypothetical, Fanali's personal marking, carried on the nose, has been documented. It consisted of a stylised dragon and the motto 'Mi Fanno un Baffo' ('I just don't care'), the emblem tracing its history back to Fanali's service in Spain where he commanded 65ª *Squadriglia Assalto*, which flew similarly-decorated Ba.65s. It also appeared on the CR.32s of 160ª *Squadriglia*, which he led in North Africa.

INDEX

References to illustrations are shown in **bold**.
Plates are prefixed 'pl.' with page numbers in brackets,
e.g. pl.**13**(52, 92)